Beneath the Southern Cross I Stand

The True Story of an Australian Soldier
told by
Darryl 'Coop' Cooper

Author: Danielle Ryan

There is a moment in the outback when the sun is setting; the sky is grey-blue with pink all around it and the sun has only just disappeared from sight... that moment of twilight where you can't be sure if it is dawn or dusk.

COPYRIGHT © 2021 BY DANIELLE RYAN

Notice of Copyright

All rights reserved. This book or any portion thereof
may not be reproduced or used in any manner whatsoever
without the express written permission of the author
except for the use of brief quotations in a book review.

Disclaimer:
Although the publisher and the author have made every effort to ensure that the information in this book was correct at press time and while this publication is designed to provide accurate information in regard to the subject matter covered, the publisher and the author assume no responsibility for errors, inaccuracies, omissions, or any other inconsistencies herein and hereby disclaim any liability to any party for any loss, damage, or disruption caused by errors or omissions, whether such errors or omissions result from negligence, accident, or any other cause.

Cover: Annie Seaton www.annieseaton.net
Background image: Shutterstock.
Front cover: Source: Adobe Stock. The soldier is an ANZAC WWI image.
Back cover: Permission granted by Southern Cross Windmills for reproduction of their brand name.

Photographs: All included photographs are the property of Darryl Cooper and Bob Frauenfelder

Printed in Australia by:
Ingram Spark, Melbourne

First Edition, 2021
ISBN 978-0-646-85322-2

This book is dedicated to Bobby 'Tags' Taylor.

Robert Taylor

Bobby was a National Serviceman who was called up for duty in the Australian Regular Army on the 13th of July 1966. Discharged on the 12th of July 1968, he then returned to civilian life. Bobby passed away on the 19th of October 2011 at 65 years of age. Dedicated in loving memory. Missed by all his mates.

Two arms, two hands, two steely bands

Under the Southern Cross I Stand,

A hero of my native land

Australia you bloody beauty! [i]

Beneath the Southern Cross I Stand

Darryl 'Coop' Cooper, Malaya, 1965.

Darryl 'Coop' Cooper

CONTENTS

Preface 7

Prelude 11

Part One. Just a Boy 13
1. My Home Town
2. Station Life
3. You'll Be Fuckin' Sorry!
4. The Recruits
5. You Start Learning Now
6. 4th Battalion of the Royal Australian Regiment (4RAR)

Part Two. The Indonesia-Malaysia Confrontation 35
7. The 28th Commonwealth Infantry Brigade
8. Terendak Garrison
9. Borneo
10. Outside the Wire
11. Inside the Outpost and Halfway Home
12. Contact
13. Back to Terendak
14. That's When It Happened

Part Three. 1st Tour Vietnam   **71**

15. 2nd Battalion of the Royal Australian Regiment (2RAR)

16. Preparation for Vietnam

17. The Vung Tau Ferry

18. The Run to Vietnam

19. 1st Australian Task Force, Nui Dat

20. 2RAR arrive at the Nui Dat Base

21. The Horseshoe

22. Back to basics at The Base

Part Four. 1st Tour Vietnam, The Operations   **97**

23. A Day at Barossa

24. Overnight in Darwin

25. The Long Green

26. Sitting Ducks

27. The Burden

28. Atherton

29. Slope 30

30. Kenmore (Ho Tram Cape)

31. Sante Fe

32. Can't See the Forest…

33. Duntroon

34. My Mate, Bones

35. Dust Off
36. The Road to Down Under

Part Five. The Long Road Home   **147**

37. The Next Bad Chapter of My Life
38. My Little Pork Pie
39. Operation Save My Life
40. Farewell again
41. Back to the Pearly Gates
42. There Were Days Like These
43. Homeward Bound
44. The End of a Chapter

Part Six. The Battle After the War   **179**

45. The Beginning of a New Chapter
46. Dawn or Dusk
47. A Final Note From 'Coop'

Acknowledgments	**190**
Bibliography	**200**
Endnotes	**201**

Darryl 'Coop' Cooper

Preface

Sometimes in life you come across someone who can brighten your day and make you laugh, no matter how terrible you are feeling. Even after all he has been through and all he has seen, this is a rare gift that Darryl has... maybe that is *because* of all he has been through and all he has seen.

Darryl and Mum met in 1992 when I was twelve years old and then spent the next twenty-six years together. I have never known what to call Darryl when referring to him – my 'Stepdad' sounded too official and didn't quite fit. A couple of years ago he sent me flowers for my birthday addressed 'To a Good Friend' which made me cry. Anyone that is friends with Darryl (any he has many) can testify to him being a true-blue good friend.

Darryl and I did not have the smoothest of starts—after all, I became a teenager shortly after they met. When I was growing up, he was suffering post-traumatic stress disorder and dealing with the horrors and nightmares of what he had gone through in Vietnam. I did not understand this at the time. I guess as we grow up and learn more about how our world works ... and with a little less naivety, we can learn to appreciate what someone has been through.

While writing Darryl's story I began researching the history of the confrontation in Borneo and the war in Vietnam. I think you need an understanding of the history to be able to write someone's story; to paint a picture and ensure it is based on true events. I read books, I watched documentaries, I trolled the net, spent countless hours reading, researching, taking notes, writing. I became bogged down in the material that is endless and could keep you reading and watching forever. There are many books on the validity of war, particularly Vietnam.

Should it have happened?

Why did it happen?

Why were the soldiers ostracised when they returned? Spat on, screamed at, beaten by citizens of their country? My research became overwhelming: the death, the destruction, the sadness, the questioning of 'why war', the unfairness of the treatment of the men put through hell. I stopped reading, I went to bed, and I slept.

I woke early to my own realisation of how I can continue to write Darryl's story…

'This is Darryl's story. Let him tell it. Just listen.'

The thing about war is that you don't have to agree with it, you don't have to understand it. The fact is it happened. I still think it is important to understand the history and politics of the time which led to the conflict; however, we won't ever truly understand the decisions of our government and I have recently learned through my research that we are never truly given all the information. The Australian public did not know about the Claret Operations in the Indonesia-Malaysia Confrontation at the time because it was subject to the British Official Secrets Act until 1996. We did not know that the bodies of our Australian soldiers were sent from Vietnam to Malaysia and our men in Malaysia had the job of burying their friends. We did not know that this was only the tip of the iceberg of what we did not know.

So rather than question, debate and politicise war, why not hear the stories of the veterans? Forget the hows and the whys and just listen. It happened, and they have endured the most horrific and heartbreaking events for our freedom. As Darryl said, "It was hard for us when we returned home from Vietnam, being spat on and called awful names, but that is why we went to Vietnam so people could express their opinion."

To that I say, "Yes, they can express their opinion, but it should be based on the truth and not assumptions or stories in the media. This is the true story of an Australian soldier."

Darryl has unlocked memories from fifty years ago to tell his story and I feel privileged to be able to write it for him. During our countless hours of discussions, we have laughed, and we have cried. When we first began, I would say, 'I can't believe I am writing a book about war.' It didn't take long for me to learn that it was never about war. It is the story of a boy, a man, a proud Australian soldier. In many ways it is a story like no other, yet in many ways it could also be the story of the 60,000 (approx.) other Australians and New Zealanders that went to Vietnam. A story of living in Australia beneath the Southern Cross—of mateship, courage, sadness and loss. A story to honour the memory of the fallen and to acknowledge those who survived but whose dreams were replaced with endless nightmares … those who still wake every day not knowing if it is dawn or dusk.

Danielle Ryan

Darryl 'Coop' Cooper

Prelude

Darryl had been digging the same hole for three hours, but it felt like three years, which is how long he'd been on the station. A long way from his home in Rockhampton and eighteen-years of age, every day the same: sweltering heat, sweat pouring, crowbar in hand, digging a hole.

Born in 1946, Darryl grew up in a time when the world was rebuilding itself following the devastation of World War II. The Cold War had begun. The war in Vietnam had started with tensions growing after Japan took over and aligned with the French. Communist forces had seized China and the war in Korea began. The "Domino Theory" was coined.

Little did Darryl know that the monotony of digging a hole was what would drive him to leave Rockhampton and join the Australian Army. That when he was fourteen years old and his principal told him he would be wasting his time if he returned to school, he would go on to have the most important job in Australia and become a soldier proud to have fought for his country. That by the time he was twenty-one, the kaleidoscope of events happening around the world meant he would be joining the war in Vietnam with 60,000 other Australians in the fight against communism that was already twenty years underway. He would no longer be digging holes for windmills, but digging holes to live in.

Over the next twenty years, he would be stationed in Malaysia, Borneo and complete two tours in Vietnam, be shot in the head and survive. He would lose his love and become a father. Those twenty years in the army, the experiences, and the comrades would turn his world upside down and be etched upon his memory forever.

Darryl 'Coop' Cooper

How could he possibly know what lay ahead? He was just an eighteen-year-old boy from Rockhampton and his story was yet to unfold.

Part 1

Just a Boy

In the outback of Australia, the silence of the land stills you. There is a moment as the sun rises that you don't move. Breathe in, the air is crisp and clean with a hint of bushland. Breathe out. Each sound, crystal clear feels like you are hearing it for the first time, every bird, every leaf rustling in the breeze. You think you can even hear each ray of light as it hits the trees and shines through onto you. Feeling the warmth of the sun as it touches your skin, you look down and can see your hands. The moment slips by. It's time to get to work.

1
My Home Town

Darryl 'Coop' Cooper grew up in Rockhampton, Australia. The area encompasses everything you picture when someone says 'Australia' or 'The Land Down Under'. The only way to describe the diversity of Rockhampton and surrounding regions is through the river upon which the town is built. Flowing through the dry outback land of Central Queensland's rural cattle stations, sheep stations and farming lands to the west of Rockhampton. Winding through many miles of mining and quarrying lands; the source of the region's gold, iron and coal. Trickling through long stretches of eucalyptus and native Australian woodlands. Twisting and turning over the Great Dividing Range through forests and the hinterland yield of tropical fruits. Finally flowing east through the urban township of Rockhampton the Fitzroy River empties into the coastal Keppel Bay and Coral Sea.

If the river could talk it would tell you of the traditional owners of the land, the Aboriginal tribes that lived on its banks. It would whisper stories of colonialism and of the battles to claim the land. It would tell tales of the British settlers who gave Rockhampton an English name after the rock formations in the river and the British village—Hampton.

Beneath the Southern Cross I Stand

In the 1850s, the town itself grew rapidly as it housed one of the biggest gold mines in the world at the time. Subsequent gold rushes meant the Fitzroy River had the second largest port in the state. The town grew fast and further migration from the United Kingdom led to the Victorian influence on Rockhampton's architecture. Prominent nineteenth century buildings like the Customs House Darryl recalls so vividly still line Quay Street giving Victorian character to the streetscape of a tropical Queensland town.

As a young boy growing up in Rockhampton in the 1950s, Darryl remembers when the ships used to sail up the river and dock at the wharves on Quay Street in the centre of town. He remembers the opening of the new Fitzroy Bridge in 1952 when he was six years old. The cutting of the ribbon by the Queensland premier was witnessed by the 30,000 people in attendance. Lights lined the streets, lit up the bridge and hung around the trees of the town hall. Celebrations continued into the evening as a band parade marched the streets and fireworks lit the sky from a barge on the river. Six-year-old Darryl looked on as everyone was dancing on the bridge.

The fifties marked a time in history that was not long after the end of World War II. The Cold War had begun. The Domino Theory had been coined by US President Eisenhower in 1954 and was the theory that underpinned the fight against communism that began in the fifties and raged for decades. The theory whereby South East Asia would fall to Communism State by State. As a result, S.E.A.T.O. (South East Asia Treaty Organisation) was formed in 1954. S.E.A.T.O was the alliance of the USA, France, Great Britain, Australia, New Zealand, Thailand, Pakistan and the Philippines formed to protect South East Asia against communist expansion.[ii] Consequently, the US involvement in Vietnam had begun and British troops were stationed in Malaya. The Menzies' government of Australia had responded with the commitment of troops to fight communist insurgencies in Korea and the Malayan Emergency.

Darryl 'Coop' Cooper

Around the time Darryl was six years old, the Korean war was underway, and the adults would talk about Korea. Darryl could never figure out what they meant about this Korea because he said, 'We were always taught growing up what our career was going to be—butcher or baker? So that's what I was thinking. These blokes are getting jobs and getting shot up.' At this age Darryl was too young to understand that this kaleidoscope of events of the fifties would ultimately shape his future and set him on a path to join the fight against communism.

Darryl's childhood was typical of the nineteen fifties in regional Australia. He was the middle of five children. His mum, Myra, cooked in hotels. If she wanted something for the house—a new fridge or carpet—she would go out and work for it. She would sew clothes and teach the girls how to sew dresses. His dad, Clarence, worked as a stockman until he got a job in town as a butcher, cutting and delivering meat to the hotels in Rockhampton. Every Saturday, Clarence would get dressed up to attend the races at Callaghan Park. On Sundays, the whole family would go to Yeppoon for picnics, and during Christmas holidays they would camp there.

Down to earth, a larrikin full of life and humour, Darryl has always had the ability to be friends with everyone. He had a lot of mates in school and grew up playing rugby league. 'When the football season came around, I was the best bloke around.' When asked what Darryl was like as a child, his eldest sister, Val said, 'The boys were larrikins.' Val would have house chores to do on a Saturday before their mum got home from work and the boys would go around, unmake the beds, and undo all her work. She ended up having to lock them out of the house and lock all the windows so they couldn't get in.

Besides football, music was Darryl's other love. Growing up, he played the piano. He says, 'My mother forced me into that. I didn't like it because I had to practise in the afternoon and my mates were out playing footy.' As a teenager he fell in love with rock'n roll music that re-defined the conservative fifties era. As rock'n roll tore through Australia from America and the Australian airwaves and jukeboxes were dominated by this new upbeat style, Darryl traded in his piano lessons for saxophone lessons. By the end of the fifties, he was slicking his blonde hair back into a quiff and listening to American artists like Bill Haley, Jerry Lee Lewis, and Chuck Berry. 'If there was a saxophone solo, I used to get into the middle of the floor and make out I was playing the saxophone.'

By fourteen, Darryl had passed his grade eight scholarship, however, he was always in trouble at school and getting the cuts from the headmaster. The headmaster told Darryl that he would be wasting his time if he came back to school and so at fourteen years of age, he left school and got a job out west on the stations.

2

Station Life

As a store boy at Southern Cross Windmills, Darryl worked out west on cattle and sheep stations around Rolleston, Springsure and Clermont. Having grown up in town, life on the stations was different. It took a full day to drive to the stations on dirt roads, so the boys lived on the station homestead or sometimes camped in tents nearby to the homestead for weeks at a time. They ate at the homestead or when they were at the tent sites, prepared their own meals. Either way, on a sheep station it was mutton for every meal. He remembers having been away for six weeks and the first meal his mother served up when he was home was mutton chops.

Darryl's love of rock'n roll music also continued out on the stations. He took his saxophone everywhere with him and would practise when he could. 'The people I used to kick around with played rock'n roll music. Every time something would come on the radio and I'm driving the car I would pull over on the side of the road and make out I'm playing the saxophone.'

His job for Southern Cross was to dig the foundations for windmills and troughs and build water tanks. It was gruelling work, and the days were long. They would start working when they could see their hands and work until they could no longer see their hands and all for six pounds a week. Relentless hours digging holes in the harsh conditions of outback Australia; hot, sweating, covered in dirt and flies. Some days so hot that his sandshoes would melt on the bottom of the tanks.

Harsh conditions and hard work aside, Darryl enjoyed his four years of station life. When they had finished building a windmill he would sit back with a cup of tea, turn on the windmill and watch as the water pumped through to the trough. He would wait and watch as the cattle and sheep came to drink from the trough, and he felt a sense of achievement.

At the time Darryl was out on the stations, global tensions were escalating and in August 1962 when he was sixteen years old the Australian Army Training Team (AATV) of thirty advisors arrived in Vietnam marking the beginning of Australia's involvement in Vietnam.[iii]

3
You'll Be Fuckin' Sorry!

Darryl loved every minute of station work but after a few years he thought there must be more out there for him. He and his mate Ken Swaddling who both worked for Southern Cross Windmills decided to take a 'sickie' to go duck shooting.

Ken now laughs, "It must have looked very suspicious! (both sick on the same day) and we were out shooting with .22s…without luck."

While out shooting, they were talking about leaving Rockhampton. They wanted to go to Brisbane to see the big smoke. Ken said, "Why don't we join the services?" Darryl thought about this and told Ken that if he was going to join it would be in the army as he had two brothers in the navy and he wouldn't join the air force. All Ken said was, "Righto we'll join the army."

The boys filled out the advertisement for servicemen in the local Rockhampton paper and took it to the Rockhampton Customs House on Quay Street. It was sent away. Not long after, Darryl received a letter advising that he needed to attend a medical in Brisbane. His mate drove him the 617 kilometres down to Brisbane. He had never left Rockhampton or the stations and says, 'When I first went to Brisbane, I could not believe how big it was and all those people in the city, it just fascinated me.'

Shortly after returning to Rockhampton at nineteen-years, Darryl received a telegram to say that he was accepted into the Australian Army. Darryl laughs, 'You could join the army at eighteen, but you couldn't be deployed overseas until nineteen and you couldn't vote until you were twenty-one.'

He received a warrant from the army to return to Brisbane. Before finalising the paperwork, Darryl and Ken had to get their parents to sign. Darryl had previously had an argument with his mum and was living out of home, so he had to confront his mum to have his papers signed. He vividly remembers the day he visited and the conversation to convince his mum to sign for him. She was not happy. With two sons already in the navy at the time, she did not want to agree – but she reluctantly signed it for him. Ken's mum did not.

Leaving from Rockhampton station, he gave the warrant to the stationmaster and boarded the train. When he arrived in Roma Street, Brisbane the army soldiers were there to pick him up and escort him to the recruiting office where there would be more exams.

He was then taken in to sign up. The sergeant said to Darryl, "How long do you want to sign for, Mr Cooper?" to which he replied, "three years." The sergeant replied, "Mr Cooper, sign for six, you will get a regular army uniform, you can go overseas, you'll have super and be well looked after."

"Yeah, that'll do me. Six years!" But it wasn't until later that Darryl laughs, 'It was all a con job as you got the same for three years as for six. So anyway, I signed for six years.'

Once signed up, Darryl swore on the Bible to protect the Queen, the country and the Governor General. As soon as the new recruits were sworn in, the officers said, "Righto, you fucking bastards, back of the truck, you're in the army now." He recalls the drive out to NCPD (Northern Command Personnel Depo) Enoggera Army Base in Brisbane on the back of that truck. A mixture of excitement and anticipation, not knowing what lay ahead, nineteen years old and miles from home.

Within the first few days in the army, Darryl had met Peter 'Andy' Anderson. Darryl was standing behind him in line at a caravan where they could get a drink. They had a drink together, and Darryl discovered his new aboriginal friend was from Mitchell, Queensland.

Besides meeting his first lifelong army friend, NCPD also taught Darryl his first lifelong army lesson. He thought, 'I'm in the army now, I'm tough!' So, he went to the mess without a shirt on, and says, 'Holy hell, didn't I get into trouble for that.' He was put on extra duties and quickly learned that he wasn't so tough after all.

Darryl would watch the soldiers marching around Enoggera and thought to himself, 'I would like to join that battalion.' There were at least one hundred of them all wearing black lanyards—that was 2RAR. They would yell out to Darryl and the other new recruits, "You'll be fuckin' sorry!"

4
The Recruits

Darryl entered the Army by himself and in February 1965 he marched into Kapooka— the recruiting and training battalion which lay nine and a half kilometres west of Wagga Wagga, New South Wales.

When he first disembarked from the bus in Kapooka, it was February and there were millions of flies, and the dust was thick in the air. They were marched onto the parade ground and stood to attention. Darryl says, 'Well, they tried to march you. As you weren't trained, you didn't know what your left foot was. We must have looked a sight!'

The recruits were issued their uniforms at Kapooka. The army didn't ask what size they were. The boys were taken to Q-Store and got what the officers wanted to give them. They threw the uniform at them, and the boys would pick their pile up and take it back to the barracks. 'You used to get back and swap with your mates to get the right size. I had a hat that I couldn't see out of. They said, that'll fuckin' do you.' The uniforms—greens, khakis, parade uniforms, boots, socks, and long johns—were meant to last their army career and that uniform went with them wherever they went. They were also given a prayer book and a white handkerchief, 'In case we had to surrender.' At Kapooka they wore a slouch hat that had the Army rising sun badge on it.

The Australian Army has firm roots in British traditions which are hundreds of years old. From the 600-page army dress code to the army law books, there is a strong history of British tradition underpinning the Australian Army. Darryl laughs, 'I think that the law books still say that if an officer is charged, he must hand over his sword and spurs.'

Recalling his time at Kapooka Darryl says now very matter-of-factly, 'Training was as hard as it could ever get.' At dawn, the bugle would sound, and the soldiers would file out on parade with their sheets folded in their arms. He laughs, 'This made us have to make our bed after we slept in it, otherwise people would just sleep on top, so they didn't have to make the beds.' They would then march back to clean the barracks. The bugle would sound again to come to the mess house hall for breakfast. They would march back to the barracks to clean again and ensure their locker was as neat as possible. If anything was a mess the Corporal would grab the locker and smash it to the floor. They would then tie their locker keys around their neck and march out to carry out drills, weapon lessons and physical training. During the end of every lesson, they had to change uniforms. At the end of the day there was no hot water so they would have a cold shower. The last bugle call would sound at ten p.m. for lights out. This went on, day in day out, for three months.

Five weeks after Darryl's arrival, Ken's mum signed his papers and he joined Darryl at Kapooka. At the time Ken had arrived, Darryl was in jail for going AWOL. The soldiers weren't allowed in the wet canteen, the "boozer" as they called it, until their fifth week drill test was passed. The drill test was the whole platoon on parade doing rifle drills for forty minutes. If the whole platoon was spot on, they would then be allowed to go to the wet canteen.

At his fifth week when the drill test was passed, Darryl and three of his mates—including Andy who he had met in Brisbane—had a couple of beers and then the canteen was closed. The boys weren't done drinking, so concocted a plan to sneak out and go into town to the pub. A group of new recruits had just marched into the training camp and the boys needed some civilian clothes for their escape, so they took the clothes from the recruits. They took the buttons off their coats and put them on to make it look like they were officers. To get into town they had to hitchhike, and they had to cross a couple of paddocks to get to the main road. As they were going through one paddock, a guard at the guard house spotted them, got in a Land Rover, and chased them around the paddock until he caught them all.

They were put in army cells which Darryl said 'Was like the inside of an icebox. All I had on was a nylon shirt and I nearly froze to death.' The next morning, they had to wake up early and rake the courtyard. They raked all the leaves down one end and the corporal would then yell, "Now rake them down the other!" This went on for some time. When they were done with the leaves, they had to polish the brass taps and nails in the shower block. Darryl overheard one of the corporals say to the officers, "Do you reckon they want to see the padre?" Darryl looked at his mates and said, "Shit, they're going to fuckin' shoot us." He really thought they were getting the firing squad for going AWOL. He says, 'From then on, I nearly got the trophy for most improved soldier.' Laughing at the memory he says, 'Fuckin' oath, I thought they were going to shoot me, I thought what's mum going to say now?'

Instead, they had to front the sergeant-major for punishment. The sergeant read out the report produced by Corporal Bob Blair who had caught them. It said that Andy was not wearing his shirt and when asked why, Andy said, "I was hot." The sergeant major told Andy, "You wouldn't be hot if you weren't running through Farmer Joe's paddocks." They were then issued with their punishment. Not the firing squad, but seven days CB (Confined to Barracks) and extra duties.

On another occasion, someone had stolen some greens, and Corporal Bobby Blair came to investigate. They all lined up at attention in the barracks. Andy's bed was across from Darryl's. The corporal came to search Andy's locker and put his hand in his great coat pocket and pulled out a handful of peanut shells. He threw them all over the floor and he said, "This is not on!" Darryl burst out laughing and the Corporal swung around to him and said "*You, Cooper, I'd like to give you a leave pass into Wagga so I can fuckin' punch the shit out of you!*" He was also the corporal who had captured them in the paddock. Darryl and Corporal Bobby Blair later became mates. They were together in Vietnam and Bob was a staff sergeant while Darryl was a digger. Kapooka marked the beginning of lifelong friendships.

There were sixty men in Darryl's platoon at Kapooka and forty of them put in for Infantry Corps. Only six got in. 'National Service was coming in and I think that the army wanted the infantry spots saved for National Service'. The army tried to put Darryl in Engineers corps and to this Darryl remembers proclaiming, "No, I'm fuckin' not." They said, "Yes, you are!" He said, "No, I'm not, I want to be a rifleman." The colonel looked at his records and said, "Cooper, you've been causing trouble here since the fifth bloody week you've been here…alright go to Infantry."

At the end of his three months in Kapooka, Darryl swore that he would never go back there again. Later in his army career, he was offered promotion after promotion to go back to train troops, but he refused. He says, 'You can shove that up your arse, no way in the world was I going back there…so that's what Kapooka was like.'

5
You Start Learning Now

Now Darryl was allocated to his Corps—the Royal Australian Infantry Corps. Private Darryl Cooper was issued with his rifle at Kapooka. This would be his rifle throughout his army career. With rifle in hand, he was moving again by train from Wagga Wagga 450 kilometres to Sydney and then west to Ingleburn "Battle Wing" for Infantry Corps Training.

Darryl says, 'Ingleburn was very different to Kapooka. You were disciplined but you were respected as you had just received a promotion from a recruit to a private.' When he got there, they marched onto parade and stood at attention. The Commander then said "Righto, everything you learnt at Kapooka, it's all bullshit. You start learning now!"

They now wore an infantry uniform—a red lanyard worn on the righthand side let people know they were Infantry soldiers, and the rising sun badge on their slouch hat was replaced with the Infantry Corps badge.

Darryl 'Coop' Cooper

There were forty men in the Infantry Training. Darryl's mate, Andy, had a bed across from him again. His mate, Roy 'Cleggie' Clegg, who turned out at Kapooka a few weeks before Darryl was already in Ingleburn when they arrived. Cleggie had to carry out duties like kitchenhand until enough men had arrived to form a new platoon. He was there for three to four weeks before Darryl got there and there were enough numbers to begin the training.

Ingleburn was three months intensive and specific training. They learned everything about shooting weapons: rifle, submachine guns, machine guns and rocket launchers. The rocket launchers were fired at old cars in a nearby field. They practised infantry tactics and contact drills. Darryl said, 'If we got a contact from the front the machine gun goes on the right or the higher ground than the rifle and then we sweep through the enemy. If we had an ambush right, we'd turn right and go straight into them. All this sort of stuff we would practice all the time.' They were also taught combat drills and bayonet drills.

There was a hall at the training grounds that was used for tear gas drills. Tear gas was thrown into the hall and the soldiers had to run in and then run out to see what damage it could do. They would do this with masks and without masks.

'It was horrible!' Darryl says, 'What the fuck did they think was going to happen!?'

A lot of the drills taught in the Australian Infantry Corps were based on those used during the Second World War. The World War II influence also extended to the weapons used. At this point in the army, the Australian soldiers were using a Bren gun which was a light machine gun that was used in the Second World War. The Bren gun Darryl carried in Borneo, was made in 1943.

They also learned about camouflage, how to get in and out of helicopters, how to dig trenches and construct overhead cover. When they weren't practising drills or learning about combat, the soldiers were undergoing physical training. The fitness programs involved endurance running, 'a twenty-mile route march' with all their gear, going over ditches, rope climbing and climbing cargo nets.

In a short three months of infantry training, there were long days to learn everything they needed to know to be in the front line and all the while they had to be immaculate in presentation. Boots polished. Brass polished. Inspected every morning and at the end of every day.

In April 1965 when Darryl was carrying out his Infantry training in Ingleburn, Prime Minister Robert Menzies announced the commitment of the first Battalion to Vietnam. 1RAR was to be deployed to Vietnam in June 1965. Darryl and Cleggie visited the Seven Hills RSL and were drinking with the men from 1RAR in May just before they had left for Vietnam.

Darryl says, 'On that particular day at Seven Hills RSL, Cleggie talked me into asking this girl to show me around Sydney and I did. That was Carol.' Carol agreed to show him around Sydney, and they began dating. In the short time they were dating, they spent a lot of time together and by the time Darryl had left Sydney they were engaged to be married.

After the three months at Ingleburn, they were then allocated to their battalion. Of the forty men training together at Ingleburn Darryl was allocated with five others to 4RAR in Adelaide. He always wanted to go to 2RAR who he watched march around the Enoggera army base in Brisbane, but he didn't mind this decision because in a couple of months 4RAR would be in Malaysia. Every two years a Battalion changed, and they were due to relieve 3RAR who were about to complete their two-year tour in Malaysia.

6
4th Battalion of the Royal Australia Regiment (4RAR)

Darryl was moving again by train with his rifle in hand. This time 1400 kilometres from Sydney to Adelaide, and then inland to the Australian Army Woodside Barracks.

When the men arrived at Woodside they were told again, "Righto, everything you learned at Ingleburn, forget it, it's all bullshit. You start learning now!"

His unit was now the 4th Battalion of the Royal Australian Regiment (4RAR). At the time there were four Battalions and the fifth was just starting. By the time the Vietnam war ended the regiment would have nine battalions. Darryl now wore the Regimental badge—the kangaroo with the cross rifles—upon his slouch hat.

The battalion was made up of four rifle Companies; A Company, B Company, C Company and D Company, commanded by the Lieutenant Colonel Thomson MC.

Each company was made up of around one hundred soldiers commanded by an Officer in Charge (OC). Darryl was allocated to B Company, commanded by Major Ducker MC, Second in Charge (2IC) Captain Bawick and Company Sergeant Major (CSM) Jock

Richardson MM. Four of the Ingleburn men went to B Company with him, including his new mates, Andy and Cleggie.

Each rifle company was then made up of three Platoons; A Company was 1 Platoon, 2 Platoon, 3 Platoon. B Company was 4, 5 and 6 Platoon. C Company was 7,8 and 9 and D Company 10,11,12 each commanded by a Major. Darryl's was the fifth platoon.

A platoon of thirty-four men were then allocated to a section of ten men each, and a hut which slept the ten men of their section.

Darryl said, 'They were World War II huts with iron walls and roofs and were freezing cold in the South Australian winter.' The hut had a single room at each end. The corporal slept at one end and the Lance Corporal slept at the other. The eight privates slept in the main room together.

Darryl was in Section 1 made up of Corporal Kinnane, who they used to call Buttons because Darryl says, 'He was always making us do up our buttons. If you were halfway up a mountain, he'd pull you up and tell you to do up your button.' Second-in-charge was Lance Corporal Don Milson who they called Butts, because in Malaysia every time they finished a smoke, he would make them take the tobacco out and then roll up the paper and bury it. Darryl and Don Milson did not get along and Andy used to call him Darryl's 'best mate'.

There were two scouts—a forward Scout and a second Scout—and a Bren gunner which was Darryl, a number two on the gun which was Andy, and the remaining four men were riflemen who included Nobby Clarke and Yogi Phillips. Cleggie was in the same platoon but in a different section to Darryl.

Darryl says, 'There were ten in your section but that was only when you didn't have any crook, wounded or killed or any away on leave or courses. It was very rare to have ten in a section. I think most of the time I was over in Vietnam in my section I only had six or seven. Most were killed or wounded.'

Darryl 'Coop' Cooper

Each soldier had a call sign based on their company, platoon and section. 'So, if you want to talk to a sun ray—a sun ray means people in charge—you ask to speak to sun ray of call sign Bravo Lima.' Darryl's call sign in Malaysia was Sun Ray of 2 2 Alfa—that's B Company, 5th Platoon, Section 1.

As well as companies A to D, the battalion was also made up of two other companies. The support company which had a mortar platoon, a sig platoon, trackers, assault pioneers etc. The other company was an administration company made up of stretcher bearers, medics, Q-store, transport platoon and cooks.

The battalion had a company headquarters which included the OC (Officer-in-Charge), the Major, the Captain, Company Sergeant Major (CSM), Staff Sergeant and his offsider.

They arrived at the platoon barracks on a Sunday. The new men entered the barracks to a party in the corporal's room. Darryl's friend, Bob Frauenfelder, says now, 'I will never forget the day that I met Coop. We were in a hut drinking beer out of the corporal's helmet. There was a knock at the door. Killer Kinnane yelled, "Come in!" and there at the door was Andy, Cleggie and Coop. Killer gives the helmet to Coop, and Coop says, "This'll fuckin' do me."' They were invited in, introduced themselves and got acquainted with their new platoon mates. Darryl remembers thinking at the time, 'Shit, we are in the regiment now.' This was the day Darryl met his good friends, Bob Frauenfelder, Yogi Phillips and Graeme Marshall.

After the first day's party had ended, Darryl remembers sitting on the side of his bed thinking the hard part was over. But says now, 'Little did I know it had just started. Loyalty, mateship, respect and the love of my country, not only Queensland but all of Australia and the Commonwealth. That's what I was responsible for now.'

3RAR had almost finished their two-year tour in Malaysia. 4RAR had eight weeks in Woodside to prepare to relieve 3RAR in October 1965. The training started and so did the medicals which involved needles and taking Malaria pills twice a day. At the end of the eight weeks at Woodside, the men were sent on two weeks' vacation leave before departing for Malaysia.

Darryl flew from Adelaide to Rockhampton. He went to see his family, visited his mates and everyone at Southern Cross. He had a cousin in 3RAR—Bob who he was about to relieve in Malaysia, so he went to visit his Aunty Hazel as well.

Darryl 'Coop' Cooper

Darryl in Kapooka

Drinking in Kapooka – Left: Ken Swadling, centre: Darryl

The boys in Kapooka – Centre: Andy

Part 2

The Indonesia-Malaysia Confrontation

In the outback of Australia, the heat is a living being. You can see it moving in waves in the air in front of you. It moves slowly past, pulsing up and down with its own beat. It rolls over you like it is alive and takes all sound as it passes. It is so heavy in the air as it wraps around you that it holds you up and hypnotises you into the same rhythm, slowing your breathing and movements as it wears you down. You can feel the beads of sweat form on your forehead and trickle down to your lip where the taste of salt lingers for a moment and then snaps you back to reality. You lift your hands clasped around the crowbar and let it drop to the earth. Lift, drop, lift, drop, lift, drop...

7
The 28th Commonwealth Infantry Brigade

Boarding the train again with his rifle, this time the trip was Adelaide to Sydney via Melbourne. The men had leave for the day in Melbourne and so dropped their weapons at the police station and visited the St Kilda RSL.

Darryl had sent a telegram ahead to Carol telling her to meet his Melbourne train at the Sydney station on his arrival. He had planned to see Carol in Sydney before he left for Malaysia. When he arrived in Sydney, Carol wasn't there. Darryl assumed she no longer wanted to see him and reluctantly went on his way.

The men stayed at Watsons Bay in Sydney for a few days. There were thirty of them due to make up numbers on a flight of engineers and their families from Sydney to Malaysia. The destination was Terendak Garrison which was fifteen kilometres from Malacca, Malaysia.

The garrison is the British version of a barracks. They were joining the 28th Commonwealth Infantry Brigade Group in the Indonesia-Malaysia Confrontation.

With a long history beginning in World War 1, the 28th Brigade was reformed several times. Australia's first involvement began when it joined the 28th Commonwealth Brigade in the fight against communism during the Korean war.

Formed again in Malaya 1955, it was then coined the 28th Commonwealth Infantry Brigade Group and its operational role was the 'Immediate Reaction Force' for S.E.A.T.O. (South East Asia Treaty Organisation), to protect South East Asia from Communist expansion.

British forces operating to defend Malaya had been operating since 1948 and were long established in the area. The Australian government committed soldiers in April 1955 when 2RAR arrived in Malaya and joined the 28th Brigade in the Malayan Emergency. From this time on, 1RAR, 2RAR and 3RAR rotated tours in Malaysia during the Malayan Emergency and 4RAR was raised and entered during the Indonesia-Malaysia Confrontation.

At the time Darryl was entering Malaysia in 1965, the brigade was now made up of the 4th Battalion Royal Australian Regiment, a battalion of Scots Guards, a battalion from the Royal New Zealand Infantry Regiment and all the supporting units from those respective countries.

The Indonesia-Malaysia Confrontation began with the opposition of Indonesia to the formation of Malaysia. Malaysia was created in 1963 by the Federation of Malaya, Singapore, Sarawak, Brunei and Sabah. President Sukarno of Indonesia saw the formation of Malaysia as neo-colonialism and with the backing of the Indonesian Communist Party (PKI) and the Indonesian Army (TNI) began attacking the Malaysian borders.[iv] The role of the 28th Commonwealth Brigade was to protect the borders from Indonesian attack.

The operations carried out in Borneo were classified and subject to the British Official Secrets Act until 1996.[v] Named the Claret Operations, Darryl says, 'We were only told what we had to do, what we were responsible for. We didn't have the big picture.

The Indonesian's used to come across the border and terrorise the villages and we were put on the border to stop that. Also, the people in Australia didn't know we were there, and we were not allowed to talk about it. We had to sign a secret agreement.' Bound by the British Official Secrets Act, the soldiers could not discuss the Claret Operations with family or friends and the Australian public was not aware of what was happening in Malaysia.

8
Terendak Garrison

In October 1965 Darryl flew from Sydney to Malaysia. He vividly remembers getting off the plane in Malaysia. He was hit in the face with the humidity and the distinct smell of Malaysia thick in the air. They were picked up by a British army truck and transported fifteen kilometres to Terendak Garrison. 'When we got to the Garrison there was a bloke there, you could call him a Salvation Army man giving out cordial—we called it lolly water—and lollies —we called them Nasho pills—but that's another story. We felt the weather; it was hot and humid.' They had to acclimatise for two weeks and weren't allowed outside of the barracks until they had done so.

Terendak Garrison was home to over 10,000 people. Not only the soldiers and the supporting units of each country's Battalions but the wives and children of any married personnel lived there also. The Garrison had 900 married quarters for them, and each family had a maid and gardener. Like a town, the Garrison was equipped with supermarket, butcher, baker, shoe repairs, tailor and hairdresser. It had churches, a cinema, pools and clubs with a bar and restaurant.

Darryl 'Coop' Cooper

Upon arrival at the garrison the soldiers were issued with British uniforms: shorts, long socks, boots and puttees. Darryl laughs remembering the British uniform, 'The shorts were flared like Bombay Bloomers, but we thought the uniforms were cool at the time.' He recalls that they used to pay five dollars a fortnight in Malay dollars (about thirty cents AUS) for boot boys who polished their boots and Dobie Wallers who washed their clothes. They were also given British webbing which they hung off their belts to carry water bottles and ammunition. The soldiers still wore the Australian slouch hat with the regimental kangaroo and cross rifle badge and had their own insignia on their shoulders so they could still be recognised as Australian soldiers. They also carried Australian weapons: Owen guns, Bren guns, SLRs and AR15s.

The sleeping arrangements at the garrison for the soldiers was much like Woodside; each section of men had their own hut. So, Darryl along with Buttons, Butts, Andy and the other men of B Company, 5th Platoon, Section 1 were allocated their hut.

Day-to-day life at the garrison involved training and preparation for deployment into Borneo. It would be six months before deployment. There was a lot of helicopter training to get used to the British helicopters: Scouts, Whirlwinds and Belvederes.

Part of the training was to learn how to jump out of moving trucks. They would go to the very back of the truck, 'run like hell' then jump out. Darryl says 'The more you ran and the faster the truck went the better because it was just like jumping out when the truck was stationary. As soon as you jump out and land on the road you would fall backwards, and you had to tuck your head otherwise you bump your head. I'll always remember old Killer Kinnane. Every time he jumped out, he forgot to tuck his head in, and he'd hit his head...every time! I'd yell out, "That'll teach you to tell me to do my buttons up, you old bastard!"'

There were jungle exercises to get used to the conditions. During this training they carried blanks and what the British called Thunder Flashes which made a loud bang like a grenade. One man from each section would carry a twenty-round magazine full of live ammunition for protection from tigers and other animals. That was the only time they carried live ammunition while training in Malaysia.

There was one particular exercise where they would be in the jungle for three weeks. They used to wear jungle boots on each exercise but this time the Officer-in-Charge made them take their marching boots along and they had no idea what for. When the three weeks had finished, the O.C. came along and said, "A Company into those trucks, C Company into those, D Company over there and B Company start walking." So that's what the marching boots were for. They were made to carry out a route march back to the garrison. It was seventy miles mostly uphill through the mountains of Malaysia. It took around three days and they had to do most of the walking at night because it was too hot during the day. The Company Sergeant Major Jock Richardson had a flagon of rum and as they fell behind in the line, he would give them a swig of rum to keep them going.

Darryl says, 'Out of 100 of us there was only one bloke who couldn't do it. It was my mate, Bones. Raymond Binning was his name, but we used to call him Bones. The only reason he pulled out was because his boots were full of blood from blisters. The marching boots were hard. Anyway, we all stuck together and looked after each other.'

Upon arrival back at the Garrison the hundred soldiers of B Company marched past the British lines singing the *Battle of New Orleans.* They then marched past the Australian lines singing *Waltzing Matilda*. The whole guard came out and presented arms as they came through the gate.

They were given a few days leave and Darryl didn't get out of bed for three days. He later found out that their Major Ducker had bet the Major of Delta Company in the officers' mess that his men could march seventy miles. Darryl says, 'Now it was Delta Company's turn he thought his D company could do better. So, off they march outside the gate. They only went about ten miles and they all packed up and marched back in. The Major of D Company was so annoyed that he ripped the Delta Company sign down and everything.'

The rivalry in the garrison didn't stop there. A rugby union competition was held between the Australian, New Zealand and the Scottish Guard Battalions. The 4RAR Commanding Officer wanted to win and took the football matches quite seriously. The Australian team gave the Scottish guards a hiding. Before the big game against New Zealand, the C.O. gave the team a month off to train. They even got all the steak at the mess with no steak allowed for anyone but the football team. The lead up to match day was serious. Darryl laughs, 'Then on the day of the match, the New Zealanders beat us sixty to nil!'

Life at the Garrison wasn't all military training. There was a social sporting club where they had cricket matches. They would go the canteen "boozer" on a Sunday afternoon which was conveniently located in front of the cricket and football grounds. When the canteen closed, they went to a little bar not far from the garrison in the jungle.

Two miles from Terendak was the local shopping strip—The Evergreen—which had a few bars. 'If you weren't on duty, you would knock off at four in the afternoon. We had a curfew of eleven p.m. We got in and out of Malacca by taxi, maybe once a week we'd go into Malacca but most of the time we'd drink just outside of the camp.'

Between the Garrison and Malacca there were around fifty bars. 'But forty-five of them were out of bounds for the soldiers. I used to always get caught out of bounds because I thought I was missing out on something.' The British red caps and the Australian military police would patrol the bars and the punishment if caught was fourteen days Confined to Barracks. He'd already been caught a few times when one night he was in a bar wearing civilian clothes which was required when they were out on leave. Darryl recalls, 'Anyway this pommy red cap came in and asked for our ID cards. We had ID cards instead of passports. I said, "I'm over here visiting from Australia." Just as I said that an Australian MP walked in and said, "Cooper! There's a cop shop over the road, I'll take you over there and you can show your passport." Another fourteen days CB.'

Between the military training and off-duty social life, the soldiers quickly established a new life at the garrison. Darryl was two months into his preparation for Borneo when he was sent a reminder of his life in Australia. He was on the parade ground when his sergeant told him that the Secretary to the Commanding Officer wanted to see him. They marched him in and asked, "Do you have a girlfriend in Australia?"

Darryl said, "No," to which they replied, "What about the one you were engaged to in Sydney?"

Carol had sent a letter to the Commanding Officer of 4RAR asking if Darryl was still there. Darryl then wrote back to Carol. It turned out that when he asked her to meet him at the Sydney train station, their wires had crossed and instead of meeting his Melbourne train in Sydney she had taken a Sydney train to Melbourne. They had literally passed each other. Carol also told Darryl the news that she was pregnant. 'She wanted to come to Malaysia to be with me at the garrison and I knew I had to do the right thing by them. The problem was that the baby would be born while I was in Borneo, and I didn't want that as Carol would be by herself at the garrison in Malaysia. I wrote her a letter saying that she shouldn't come there. She had got the wrong idea thinking I didn't want her anymore and we broke off.'

9
Borneo

On Anzac Day, the 25th of April 1966, the men of A and B Company 4RAR boarded the British troop ship carrier, the *Auby*. The destination was Kuching, the capital of Sarawak, North Borneo. They departed from Port Dickson, and it would be a three-day journey. Joined by attachments of British commandos, the time was passed with a euchre competition onboard and Darryl and his partner, Yogi Phillips, came in second place.

C and D Company boarded another ship which had departed two days earlier, the *Sir Lancelot*. The conditions on the two ships were very different. Darryl laughs, 'On the *Auby* you couldn't lean on the safety rails because it was all rusted through and you would end up in the South China Sea. It had been salvaged about three times this boat. The *Sir Lancelot* had a picture theatre. We drew the short straw; it was probably the officers gambling up in the mess again.'

On arrival in Kuching the men then went by trucks to an area just outside of Bau where the 4RAR Battalion headquarters was located. 4RAR was now taking part in the Claret Operations and was responsible for the forty miles of the border with Indonesia which was essentially just a creek and mountains. All the training in Australia and in Malacca over the last year had prepared the men for this tour in Borneo.

C Company remained in reserve at the battalion headquarters and the other three rifle Companies, A, B and D, were deployed to separate outposts near the border. Over the course of time spent in Borneo C Company relieved A and D companies so they could have a break from the outposts. B Company was not so lucky and remained at their outpost the whole time. Darryl speculates, 'It was probably the officers gambling up in the mess again.'

B Company travelled to Stass where they would be stationed 1000 meters from the border. A company's outpost was at Gumbang and D Company at Bokah. There were no roads between Bau and the outposts, so the men had to be choppered in via Belvederes which carried around twenty men at a time. They were also resupplied at the outpost by chopper and parachute. Darryl recalls, 'They would parachute our ammunition and rations in. A "roman candle" is where the chute doesn't open and just falls straight to the ground. It only used to happen on our beer rations, and we thought the Poms used to do that to pay us back.'

Commanded by Major Ducker, 2IC Captain Barwick and CSM Jock Richardson, B Company arrived at their outpost in Stass. They relieved a company of Ghurkas. Being located in the middle of the jungle, the living conditions were primitive. They slept in bunkers underground which, on arrival, had to be fumigated due to bugs. The mess and company headquarters were above ground. They had cooks, stoves, army shower buckets and importantly a boozer where they could sign for two cans of beer a day. Darryl says, 'We were only allowed canned beer, no stubbies because we could cut ourselves on the glass. Don't worry that we are in a war zone.'

10

Outside the Wire

The soldiers wore Australian bush hats out on patrol. B Company had a blue cross on their hats, A Company, a yellow circle, and D Company, a red cross. This was to identify the company so the other soldiers of 4RAR patrolling the border would not engage their own men.

Now they are in Borneo they carried live ammunition; Claymore mines and pineapple grenades that were used in the Second World War. They would go out on patrol with ten days rations, sleeping gear, mines, ammunition, grenades, batteries and cigarettes. Fully loaded with gear they would need to lighten the load where possible. Darryl laughs, 'Milson (Butts) cut off the handle of his toothbrush to lighten the load and I said to him, "Why'd you do that? No way I'm doing that, how the fuck are you going to brush your teeth?"'

During the rainy season, they didn't worry too much about water out on patrol as it would rain every night and the creeks would supply ample water until they returned to the outpost. They carried a special tablet to clean the water to be able to drink it safely. The problem was in dry season when they were patrolling the mountains and the creeks weren't flowing it was difficult to find water. They would have to ration the water by drinking out of the bottle cap.

Two platoons would go outside the wire on patrol—the wire is the perimeter of the outpost and it zigzagged around the outpost. One platoon would stay back at the outpost and then they would swap over. They left the outpost on patrol for seven to ten days at a time and would patrol with their platoon and always with their section. In Darryl's section (1) Ollie Olsten was out front as their scout. Ollie Olsten was already in Malacca when 4RAR came over; he was left over from 3RAR. Then Corporal Kinnane (Buttons) was behind Ollie, Darryl (Bren Gunner) behind the Corporal, Andy (second on gun) behind Darryl, next is the rifleman; Nobby Clarke and Yogi Phillips and at the rear is second-in charge, Don Milson (Butts).

During the patrols in Borneo, there was only one scout in Darryl's section. Darryl explains, '2RAR (in Vietnam) had different tactics to what 4RAR had in Borneo. Being in jungle that thick we only used the one scout so we wouldn't lose contact with him. The tactics would also change depending on who we were fighting. For example, in Vietnam the Viet Cong were different to the NVA because the Viet Cong were guerrillas, and the North Vietnamese Army were well trained soldiers.'

The country of Borneo was an expanse of either mountains and jungle or swampland near the rivers. The jungle was thick, and they had to hack their way through it with machetes. This made patrolling by foot a slow and difficult process. Sometimes they would come across a rubber plantation which was open country and a welcome break. The creeks throughout the countryside would often be flooded and to get over the creeks they would use a log. Darryl said, 'Every time I'd cross over on the log, I'd fall off with all the gear I was carrying. It would happen just before dark so you couldn't dry your gear out.'

Being in thick, remote and secluded jungle always posed a high risk of losing contact with each other. At any time during patrol, each man had to make sure he could see the man in front of him. This would always keep the section together. Some nights without any moon they couldn't see their own hand in front of them so there was no chance of seeing the man in front. The leaves of the jungle floor had become phosphorescent over the years so they would put the leaves on the back of their pack to be able to see each other.

Additionally, Lance Corporal Milson at the back would carry a map and compass. If any riflemen got lost or disorientated, Donnie Milson would be there with a map and compass to get them out. Darryl wasn't sure that he was up to this task. There was one patrol where they were in the dark and had to get back to the right side of the border. 'Killer was acting Sergeant at the time and Milson was our Commander, and I am carrying the gun and all this shit and anyway I come across this tree and I said, "Geez I'm pretty sure I've seen that tree before" and I said to Andy "I'm going to kill that bastard! He's taking us around in circles" Which he was. I used to be a Sig Commander; I know how to read a map. He should have been able to. Three times we went past this tree. Must have been a couple of hours…and it was in the swamp too!'

On some patrols, they would head directly outside the wire of the outpost to start patrol. Other times there may have been reports of movement in a particular area so they would be choppered in to search that area.

On one particular patrol, they were going outside the wire by foot. As they step outside the wire, they cock their weapons ready for action. Darryl cocked his weapon and then heard a big bang. 'Luckily enough Killer Kinnane had just gone around the corner otherwise he would have had his foot blown off. Anyway, our OC was there,

Major Ducker, and he was yelling out "Charge that man! Charge that man!" I was looking around thinking who was that dickhead? We had that much gear on Andy had to come and put his knee in my back and cock the weapon. I looked in front of me and there was a big hole. It was my weapon that went off. As soon as that happens it is twenty-eight days loss of pay. So, I'm thinking shit I'm going out to get shot and won't get paid.'

When they got back to the outpost the armourer had to check the weapon. What they discovered was that the breach didn't come back far enough to lock in the firing position. The bolt just moved forward, picked up a round out of the magazine and fired it. The cause was a worn-out cocking sear which was the trigger mechanism. Luckily for Darryl, he got paid.

In addition to their own men, they would patrol with men from local tribes who would assist as interpreters and border scouts. Sarawak was made up of two tribes – the Ibans and Dyacks. The Ibans were hunters who lived in the jungle and the Dyacks, fishermen living close to the sea and rivers. A number of men from these tribes volunteered to the Malaysian Army and were then allocated to the 28th Brigade. The Ibans carried a shotgun but also a sandbag on the back of their pack along with a *Parang*, which is the Malaysian word for knife. It looked much like a machete. For a long time, Darryl didn't know what the sandbag was for. Towards the end of their time in Borneo he found out, 'One day we were going to attack the Indonesians, but they had just started the peace talks in Jakarta, so we weren't allowed to attack. This Iban went off his brain. He wanted to use the sandbag to take the heads of the Indonesians back to the village. He was upset he wasn't given the chance.'

Most of B Company's patrols were in the Gunaria mountains. Darryl says, 'Andy was always by my side. He's been with me since the beginning in Brisbane. At Kapooka and Ingleburn his bed was across from me and in Borneo he was now second on gun.'

They would always give each other a hard time and in the midst of everything they were going through would still have a laugh. Darryl says, 'I would be climbing a mountain with a machine gun and Andy would say, "Here let me carry that for a while." I would say, "No I'm right." Then three-quarters of the way up I'd say to Andy, "Can you carry this now?" Andy would go off, "You bludging bastard, you had to wait until now!" Then we would get to the top and would be digging in and I would say to Andy, "I have to go to the toilet," Andy would go off again, "You bludging bastard, you better bring some back on a stick as proof!"'

Out on patrol they would sleep on the side of the mountains. To be able to sleep on the mountain and off the ground of the jungle they would cut down small saplings and lay them parallel to make stretchers out of them. When they were in the swamps they had to sleep up in trees and would to tie themselves up in the tree amongst the swamp so they wouldn't fall out when they fell asleep. There were times that they didn't have to tie themselves up. Darryl explains, 'You'd be up there like a koala in between the forks of the tree.' The rainy season made these sleeping conditions even more difficult. 'By the time it was last light, we would try to hoochi up by 4 p.m. because that's when the storms used to come, monsoons. The hoochi was made of plastic like a poncho and would be set up with a mosquito net like a tent to cover you. Also, the mosquitos wouldn't bite you in the hoochi, they would carry you outside to bite you. To boil the billy, you had to have the stove outside in the rain. It was wet and miserable.'

When they slept in the trees there would be no cover from the monsoons.

Other times they would receive shelter in a village along the way. The British army looked after the villagers in Borneo helping them with medical assistance or building roads. 'They called it *Operation Hearts and Minds* and anything they could do for the villagers they would. We used to go to the villages and take medics with us and the medics would look after the sick. The locals loved us.'

Darryl recalls one village they went into was so secluded they hadn't seen white men since the Second World War when the Australians were fighting the Japanese. B Company entered the village just on last light; they could see eyes peeping out of the huts. One section camped on the track into the village and another section camped on the track out of the village ready to ambush any enemy. A Dutch missionary took Darryl's section to a meetinghouse in the middle of the village where they slept for the night. First light the next morning they woke and looked up to see skulls hanging from the ceiling above them. 'They say they were the heads of Japanese soldiers from World War II.' For the men of B Company, it was a sobering realisation they were patrolling areas deep in the middle of remote jungle amongst primitive tribes and villages and were nowhere near civilisation.

11

Inside the Outpost and Halfway Home

Patrol in Borneo was gruelling; fully loaded with gear, dense jungle, harsh weather and sleeping conditions. It taught the men jungle warfare that prepared them for Vietnam, yet Darryl says, 'Borneo wasn't like Vietnam. In Borneo the patrols were harder. In Vietnam everything was on a silver platter—if you wanted anything, they'd give it to you. If you wanted water, you'd ring up the helicopters and they'd bring it to you—or if you wanted rations or ammo. In Borneo you had to carry everything yourself and you had to live off what you had on you and the land around you.'

In between patrols, B Company would return to their outpost at Stass where they would have a break anywhere from two days to a week. Patrol, outpost, patrol, outpost, patrol, outpost. This went on for five months.

The Company Sergeant Major of B Company—Jock Richardson looked after his men. Darryl said of Jock, 'Best CSM I had in the army. He was a real sad, old bloke. He used to hate us going out because he thought we wouldn't all be coming back. Every night Jock would come around and ask how we were going.'

There was a small creek going through the outpost and while the men were out on patrol Jock had the pioneers build a small bridge across the creek made of bamboo to look like the Sydney Harbour Bridge.

Every day, the men would "stand to" for around twenty minutes before dawn and twenty minutes after. They would also "stand to" twenty minutes before sunset and twenty minutes after. This was done based on the tactics of their enemy. The enemy would sneak up during the night and attack on first light and at the end of the day the enemy would attack just before sunset and sneak away at in the dark of the night. Consequently, the men had to "stand to" at dawn and dusk prepared for battle. There was a British 105mm artillery Howitzer on the outpost, and at last light they would fire the Howitzer along the border to warn off the enemy. Darryl recalls at "stand to" he would be in the trench with his rifle and ammo waiting for the enemy to attack. Everything was dead quiet, looking out onto their miniature Sydney Harbour Bridge. The Howitzer would fire, and he would hear the sound of jets and look up to see the British Hunter jets flying overhead looking for any large enemy mass. They would do this every day, at dawn and dusk.

The short breaks at the outpost were a welcome reprieve from the patrols. On one of the breaks the soldiers were taken from the outpost up the river to a little beach to go skiing. They stayed there for two days and had a canteen where they could drink as much as they want. 'The officers must have won a bet,' Darryl says.

Another time, Col Joy and the Joy Boys arrived with Little Pattie to entertain the men. Darryl says, 'We had a ball. They left there and went straight to Vietnam to play. That's when about two weeks later on the 18th of August in Vietnam 6RAR was in the Battle of Long Tan.'

During their time in Borneo, B Company would stay across what was happening in Vietnam via a radio at the outpost. There were many days where the men would crowd around the radio to listen to the latest news. The Royal Australian Regiment had two battalions in Vietnam at the time and there was talk of sending another one. It was going to be 4RAR straight from Malaysia but that never eventuated. The men of 4RAR were frustrated—they were listening to the news in Vietnam and hearing of their friends being killed in battle. They wanted to help.

12
Contact

During the previous year in 1965, the cross-border operations were more aggressive and 3RAR had undertaken several successful ambushes. At that time the platoons were authorised to cross the border into Kalimantan up to 7000 metres.[vi]

Once the peace talks had started, the Claret operations were then limited to surveillance and contact was to be avoided where possible, therefore, 4RAR did not conduct aggressive cross-border raids and consequently did not experience the same level of conflict as their predecessors. Darryl says, 'There was little contact with the Indonesians on patrol. It was more frustrating not having contacts than having them. It was like learning to drive a car then not being able to drive a car. We never went looking for them, we just expected they'd come to us. But we were doing our job patrolling—they were scared of us.' Darryl believes that the Claret Operations and their patrol of the border made a difference; their presence kept the Indonesians at bay and consequently prevented village invasions.

During patrols, the soldiers used to get alerts of amber, red and green alert which indicated the level of enemy in a particular area and what alert they needed to be on. If an area was high alert, they would have to "dig in" to be ready to attack. This meant using the trenching tool they carried to dig a shell scrape. A shell scrape is essentially a hole which is eighteen inches deep and as long as their body. They would lay in the hole and be under ground level and out of sight. "Digging in" was always hard work and in Borneo it was harder; there were always tree roots to cut through. Once the job was done, they would lay in their shell scrape on alert.

On one particular day Darryl and his section were heading to the border to get water from the creek which was only a couple of metres wide, ankle-deep and separated Indonesia from Malaysia. As they approached the creek directly across from them and only a couple of metres away stood an Indonesian soldier. He was getting water too. Darryl says, 'He looked up at us and his bloody eyes nearly popped out of his head. I swung my weapon around and we just looked at each other. He got up and moved away, and I moved away. It might have been a different story if he was on our side of the creek, or I was on his.'

On another occasion Darryl says, 'There was one village we went into we just missed the CCO which was the Chinese Communism Organisation—the guerrillas. A mother brought this child over to us—five or six-years old. What they had done was they hacked the top of his instep with a machete and his foot was hanging off the bone, so we immediately got a helicopter in and took him and his mother out. I didn't hear any more about it. They were doing shocking things. We tried to chase them. For a day and a half, we went up these mountains chasing these bastards, but we couldn't get them because they knew the area.'

The biggest conflict that happened for 4RAR during their tour in Borneo was with C Company. The day of the contact the officers had given B Company a rest from patrolling the Gunaria mountains and let them patrol the foothills so they wouldn't have to go up into the mountains. B Company had spent months up in the Gunarias and this was the first day that they were down the bottom. 'It was just on last light at "stand to" and all hell had broken loose. C Company was up the mountain and they had come across the enemy. The enemy were sitting there waiting to ambush them. I think they killed about three or four of the enemy and they lost one of our blokes—Bob Frauenfelder's best mate, Viv Richards, died from his wounds. There was also another bloke wounded—Eddie Lang—"tough as nails" we used to call him. They wouldn't let us go up to give them a hand…we call that the Battle of the Gunarias.'

13

Back to Terendak

On the 11th of August 1966 a peace settlement was reached between Malaysia and Indonesia and all non-Malaysian troops in Borneo had to be withdrawn within twenty-eight days. This was no small task, given there were around 20,000 troops in Borneo. There was exception made for Australian engineers constructing roads in Sabah.[vii] 4RAR was to head back to the base of the 28th Commonwealth Infantry Brigade Group at Terendak Garrison, Malacca.

Before they withdrew out of Borneo, 4RAR had to conduct what they call "yippee shoots" to dispose of ammunition. They had to fire ammunition at targets into the jungle. Darryl says, 'The whole platoon was out doing this so that's about thirty blokes and we had all these two-inch mortars we had to fire off.'

They were firing over the wire into the front of their position.

'We must have fired about half a dozen and this one particular mortar fizzled out of the barrel, went up in the air and everyone just looked at each other until someone ran, then we all ran.' The mortar came down and landed on Company Headquarters roof and the Major, Captain and Lieutenants were all in there. Luckily enough it didn't go off - the mortar had to go a certain distance and so many rotations before it arms itself. Darryl said, 'At the time my mate, Graeme Marshall, was giving us grid reference and when the mortar landed Graeme yelled out "Up five miles!"'

In September 1966, B Company 4RAR once again boarded the old British troop ship carrier the *Auby*. 'The officers must have lost another bet in the officers' mess.' Bound for Singapore, this time they were joined by a company of New Zealand soldiers and a company of English soldiers. On the trip back, the men were allowed to have a few drinks. Halfway home and a few drinks in, Darryl says, 'The Poms and the Kiwis started arguing and we Aussies were sitting on the side. Now and again the Poms would start singing *Waltzing Matilda* to try and get us on their side and then the Kiwis would sing *Click Go the Shears* so we would side with them.'

Tensions were high and a huge fight was anticipated.

Darryl says, 'And there was a big blue, but it was Aussies fighting Aussies over who they were going to back. One bloke yells, "You were backing the Poms!" and another, "You were backing the Kiwis!" and it was on. All hell broke loose. After that it was a dry boat for the rest of the trip back.'

The *Auby* berthed in Singapore. The English and New Zealand soldiers disembarked and went their separate ways. B Company 4RAR was greeted by the British red caps guarding the gangway so that they couldn't get off. It seemed because of their antics on the trip back that they had gained a personal military police escort back to Terendak. They were not allowed to disembark until the next morning. The Ghurkas took them in trucks to the Singapore railway station where they were escorted by the military police on the train back to Malacca. They then changed over to another truck escort and headed back to Terendak.

14
That's When It Happened

Back at the garrison it was back to training and physical fitness mixed in with some Rugby and visits to the canteen.

Darryl expected to go straight to Vietnam from Malaysia because there were only two battalions in Vietnam at this stage (5RAR and 6RAR) and there was talk of another one going over. The men of 4RAR were sure they were being prepared to complete a tour in Vietnam. There were even American officers arranged to speak with the 4RAR soldiers at the Terendak base. One company at a time, the men filed into a room to listen to the officers speak. The officers recounted their version of what happened and how the war in Vietnam all started. There was a long history in Vietnam beginning with the Japanese, French and now US involvement. At the time there were nearly 200,000 US troops in Vietnam.[viii]

Darryl said, 'The US officers spoke to us about the Viet Cong, and they had a film of the Viet Minh when they beat the French in the battle at Dien Bien Phu. They spoke about all the things that were happening in South Vietnam and why we were going there, so they could have safe relations in the South.' It was the first time the men of 4RAR had an understanding of why the war in Vietnam was occurring and why they were needed.

Darryl didn't need American officers trying to persuade him to fight in Vietnam. He already had his own motivation. One of Darryl's main duties back at the Garrison was being on funeral detail for soldiers killed in Vietnam. Darryl says, 'If a soldier's family in Australia couldn't afford to send their body from Vietnam back to Australia, the government flew the deceased to Malaysia where the men of 4RAR would hold a funeral. There is a photo of Andy and me. We are sitting in the back of a Land Rover (pg 68). I used to hold all the hats for the pallbearers. Andy sat across from me. It wasn't a very nice thing, but we made it respectable for them.' This went on for a couple of months. Darryl assisted with around six burials. Darryl and Bob Frauenfelder visited Malaysia a few years ago. Darryl says 'There are still Australians buried there from Vietnam now. Just before we went over, there was a big stink about it. The Australian War Graves resumed most of the bodies and brought them back to Australia.'

The next six months at the Garrison was a mix of the old routine: training, fitness, rugby, canteen mixed with the new role of funeral detail and all the while being one step closer to Vietnam. 'We were getting sigs from Vietnam, and it was on the ABC news. We heard about a lot of the battles, and we knew it was bad over there. We wanted to go over because our mates were getting killed. We were sitting on our arses with peace in Malaysia and what were we doing…you know…we could be over there helping. That's the way we looked at it.'

That's when it happened. Darryl remembers it clearly. The men of B Company 4RAR were walking across a field after just finishing a game of rugby against the English. 'We gave them a hiding,' Darryl says. They were in high spirits. Captain Bawick was waiting for them. He gathered them together and he said, "You, you, you, you can go" and "You, you, you derros can stay here." Pointing to the first lot he said, "You blokes will be sent back to Australia, to Brisbane where you will go down to Kapooka, be promoted to corporal and become instructors for the National Service. For you derros (which was Darryl's group) you go back to Australia, join 2RAR and go straight to Vietnam."'

Darryl said, "You beauty!" and they went to the boozer.

At that stage all soldiers in 4RAR had all their gear packed ready to go anywhere in the world within forty-eight hours. Darryl says, 'Our trunks were packed at all times with all our gear at the front of our bed and the CSM and sergeant used to come and inspect them to make sure we had everything.' At least one company had to be on duty at all times so if you were the duty company you had to stay in and had a curfew of ten p.m. The duty officers used to go around and complete a roll call to make sure everyone was home. Darryl laughs, 'After hearing the news that we would be sent to Vietnam, this one particular day our whole platoon was out on the piss and they sprung one of these roll calls and the whole platoon got charged.'

All in all, eight men got promoted from private to corporal and went to Kapooka as instructors. Sixty men including Darryl went from 4RAR and joined 2RAR. Andy was in hospital at the time and so didn't get to go; he went to Vietnam with 4RAR later on. During Darryl's tour in Borneo 2RAR was split in half to make 6RAR. 'At the Battle of Long Tan, most of those blokes were 2RAR blokes because they had split from 2RAR to form 6. That's one of the main reasons we were sent back. To reinforce 2RAR.'

4RAR left Malaysia homeward bound to Australia on the 19th of March 1967.

Darryl says now, 'After Borneo I look back at the really hard times, we had but we endured through it. We didn't realise how much the mind and body could take but we all made it. We lost a couple of blokes over there. I was very proud to say that I fought with the British army; they are fair dinkum. Looking back now, Borneo was the hardest part of my twenty years of army life.'

Entering the main gate at Terendak Garrison

Terendak Barracks

B Company on parade at Terendak

Terendak – Funeral for a Vietnam Veteran. Darryl and Andy in back of truck

4RAR on parade at Terendak

4RAR band on parade at Terendak

Darryl 'Coop' Cooper

Football at Terendak

Terendak sports club. From left: Gary Easton, Cleggie, Andy, Bob Frauenfelder, Keith Heavey, Darryl, Max Cannan, Yogi Phillips, Kev Rideout

Andy and Darryl

Andy at the barracks

Supply drop at Stass

Boarding 'the Auby', 25 April 1966, Port Dickson. Darryl, front right, with gun on shoulder.

Bunkers at Stass – Gunaria Mountains in background

Darryl 'Coop' Cooper

Darryl says, 'On a twenty-miler'. Darryl front right, Cleggie behind him

Sharing out rations on patrol in Stass. Darryl back left

River crossing out on patrol. Darryl says, 'Just before I fell in.'

Local tribesmen in Borneo

A village in Borneo

Mortar at Stass

105 Howitzer at Stass – Tower and wire in background

Machine gun looking outside the wire at Stass

Darryl 'Coop' Cooper

Listening to the Melbourne Cup in the bunkers at Stass.

Listening to records at the barracks, Terendak. Left: Cleggie, Max Cannon asleep. Right: Darryl, Graham Marshall

Center: Darryl, Little Pattie, Cleggie, Graham Marshall, Max Cannon

From Left: Killer Kinane, taxi driver, Knobby Clarke

Terendak – Christmas dinner 1966

Going on leave after Borneo – KL airport to Penang 1966. Darryl front centre, right, Bones Binning.

Part 3

1ˢᵗ Tour Vietnam

Just before a storm everything becomes still. The air is heavy…. humid. Beads of sweat appear on your face even though you are not moving. Your senses heighten; you breathe in the smell of rain coming, you see the black and grey clouds, ominous as they roll across the whole sky. On the ground, nothing is moving, there is not a breath of air and not a sound.

As the storm gets nearer the breeze picks up and everything takes on the rhythm of that wind; the trees all around gently move in unison, the door to the tin shed slowly creeks back and forth, the windmill begins slowly clicking over, the homestead whistles as the wind passes around it.

15
2nd Battalion of the Royal Australian Regiment (2RAR)

19th March 1967, Darryl along with sixty-seven other soldiers from 4RAR boarded a British flight in Malaysia—British Eagles homeward bound for Australia. The men enjoy a few beers at the stopover in Singapore for an hour. Back on the plane spirits are high and the celebration continues. Darryl says, 'Halfway home, the pilot left the cockpit door open and here's the air hostess up on his lap kissing him. We all cheered, and they cheered back. We had a ball! Before getting home, I was thinking to myself I wonder what Australia is going to be like, I've been away for a couple of years, and we got back, and decimal currency happened while I was away in 1966. We knew that Australia had gone to decimal currency, but we didn't know when or how or what it looked like. We were fighting a war and worried about our mates in Vietnam. At one point, I was sitting there looking out of the window of that flight thinking I am going to 2RAR. It took me back to when I first joined the army at NCPD, Enoggera when I was watching 2RAR marching with their black lanyards.'

Where 4RAR was raised in 1964 on the Adelaide oval just prior to deployment in Malaysia, the 2nd Battalion was raised just after the second world war in Borneo. At the time the 34th Australian Infantry Brigade which was raised in 1945 had three battalions: the 65th, 66th and 67th Battalions. After the Second World War, volunteers were called for soldiers to stay in the army and be deployed for duty and rehabilitation of Japan. A Battalion in the 9th Division—the 66th Battalion became the 2nd Battalion of the Australian Regiment (2AR). The 65th Battalion was in the 6th Division, and they became 1AR. The 67th Battalion in the 7th Division became 3AR. The Royal title was granted in March 1949.

At that time 3RAR went straight to Japan, 2RAR were posted in Puckapunyal and 1RAR was posted at Ingleburn. In 1950, 3RAR were sent to Korea where they were attached to the 27th British Commonwealth Brigade.[ix] Two years later 1RAR joined them in Korea as part of the 28th British Commonwealth Brigade and in 1953 2RAR replaced 1RAR in Korea. Darryl says, '3RAR ended up winning a presidential citation over there. When they formed the Royal Australian Regiment, they were called "old faithful" because you could always depend on 3AR.' They had served in Japan and then served the whole war in Korea—four years.

When Darryl was first in the army at Enoggera watching 2RAR on parade and marching around the grounds, he always wondered why they had a black lanyard. 1RAR had a blue lanyard, 3RAR a green lanyard, 4RAR had a red lanyard. He later found out that when 2RAR were presented with their drums, King George VI had died so as a mark of respect for King George VI, 2RAR blackened their drums, their belts, their gators and wore a black lanyard. Their nickname was the 'Black Drummers'.

16
Preparing for Vietnam

After arriving back from Borneo, Darryl had leave to go home to see his family. He says, 'I headed home to Rockhampton, and I didn't know what to expect.' He had not told anyone he was coming home. When the taxi dropped him off on his street, nobody was home. 'The lady from next door came over and invited me over for a cup of tea. She had an old Queenslander, and I was up on the porch having a cup of tea with her. We could see down the end of the street to the corner. The neighbour told me Dianne, my younger sister, should be coming home from high school soon. I was still in my army uniform. I noticed three or four girls up at the corner. I stood up and the next thing I heard was a shout, "My army brother! He is home!" She ran down the road crying and calling my name. She gave me the biggest hug ever.'

'Not long after that my parents came home, and we had a bit of a reunion with a couple of beers. Later that night I told them that the bloody war in Vietnam was getting worse and I told them that the army wanted me to go there with 2RAR and fight in the Australian uniform. They were not impressed for I had been away in Malaysia for nearly two years. But when I left, they gave me their blessing. Don't forget that when I left, I had two brothers away in the navy, so they had no sons left at home.'

Darryl and the other soldiers arrived back at Eagle Farm—Brisbane airport—and were trucked out to 2RAR who were stationed at the Enoggera barracks. At this time all soldiers going to Vietnam had to undertake a course in jungle warfare and the soldiers of 2RAR had just been through these exercises. Darryl and the other men from 4RAR already had their experience from two years in the jungles of Malaysia.

Upon arrival at Enoggera, they disembarked the trucks and assembled behind battalion headquarters which was essentially an old house in the middle of Enoggera where the colonels and majors used to be. Darryl says, 'We used to call it Bullshit Castle.'

The soldiers were then asked what company and platoon they wanted to go to. Cleggie was with Darryl at the time. He went to Assault Pioneers. Darryl went to B Company, 4th Platoon.

The men were marched to their particular barracks. It was a weekend and there was no one there except for Lance Corporal Bill Parry. Darryl says, 'I can always remember Bill Parry. He was the first bloke in B Company that I met. He had tattoos all over him. He allocated us a bed and what section we were in.'

Darryl and the other men spent a week at their new barracks and were then sent on two weeks pre-embarkation leave. He returned to Rockhampton to say goodbye to his family and his friends at Southern Cross Windmills. He clearly remembers the advice from the old guys at Southern Cross Windmills. They had been in World War II and their parting words to him were "Keep your head down mate."

After pre-embarkation leave, it was back to Enoggera Barracks. Darryl marched into his new platoon. He was now officially in 4th Platoon, B Company, Section 2.

Darryl 'Coop' Cooper

It was time to get acquainted with company headquarters and meet the other members of 4th Platoon:
*NB This is not a full and comprehensive list of the Battalion, however, those relevant to Darryl's story and those that he can remember given it was fifty years ago are included.

Battalion Headquarters:
Commanding Officer (CO) – Lt Col N.R. 'Chicka' Charlesworth
Second in Command (2IC) – Major D.V. Smith
Regimental Sergeant Major (RSM) Warrant officer 1st class R.L. Moon

B Company:
Officer Commanding (OC) – Major William 'Maps' Carter
Second in Command (2IC) – Captain Jeremy Taylor
Company Sergeant Major (CSM) – Warrant officer 2nd class Marco 'Kiwi' Gibbons
Q Store Sergeant (CQMS) – Sergeant George Catacos

4th Platoon:
Platoon Commander – Lieutenant 1st class Kevin McTaggart. Replaced during the 1st tour by Lieutenant 1st Class Jim Connolly.
Platoon Sergeant Jack Woods. Replaced during the 1st tour by Sergeant Tom Birnie.

Section 1:
Corporal Ian Atkinson
Lance Corporal Richard 'Dicky' Glenn. Dicky was 4th intake of National Service
Private Stan 'The Man' Jaruga
Private Selwin Pitt
Private David Whitehouse

Beneath the Southern Cross I Stand

Private John 'Johnny' Barnes (came from 4RAR also)

Already in Vietnam from 6RAR:
Private Bill 'Billy' Wearne
Private Robert Carmichael
Private Bob 'Bobby' Taylor

Section 2: (Darryl's Section)
Corporal Brian 'Andy' Andrews
Lance Corporal Sandy Sanderson
Private Ralph Hoger (machine gunner)
Private Darryl Cooper (number 2 on gun)
Private John 'Johnny' Beggs (scout) (4th intake of National service)
Private Alan Victor 'Bluey' Jaques. Darryl says, 'Bluey was the 'Arse end Charlie'. He was really proud of being Arse End Charlie old blue.' Bluey was 4th intake of National Service.

Already in Vietnam from 6RAR:
Private George 'Georgie' Duff
Private Alan Carter
Private Mick Pinkus

Section 3:
Corporal Bob Murray
Lance Corporal Bill Parry
Private Kerry Pierce (came over from 4RAR with us)
Private Robert Klopp

Already in Vietnam from 6RAR:
Private Angus Richardson
Private Denis Wanless

** The men who came in as reinforcements (reos) from the fourth intake of National Service went home early as they only had two years of National Service.

4 Platoon, B Company, 2RAR. (Darryl not in photo as he was on leave at the time)

These were the sections when 2RAR had left Australia for Vietnam. Darryl says, 'Now we got a few soldiers over there who stayed over for us because they were "reos" and got there late with 6RAR and one of them was my mate, Bobby Taylor; Bobby was a Nasho.'

National Service was introduced from the early 1900s. Refined, debated and re-introduced a number of times, by 1964 the fourth scheme introduced via the National Service Act 1964 meant that conscription of twenty-year-old males was compulsory, and they were chosen via a lottery draw based on their date of birth. Once chosen they had to serve two years in the Regular Army and three years part-time in the Regular Army Reserve.

Beneath the Southern Cross I Stand

The fourth National Service scheme was introduced at the time Darryl was involved in the Indonesia-Malaysia Confrontation and when 1RAR was deployed to Vietnam. At this time, the Menzies government increased the commitment to Vietnam and the scheme was introduced with the aim of increasing army strength to 40,000 full-time soldiers.[x]

Darryl says of National Service, 'I think the first intake went with 1RAR to Vietnam and the second intake came to us in Malaysia. One of the blokes that came to us, I went to school with. A bloke by the name of Dusty Miller. The second intake came to Borneo, and we only had about five in the company. Not sure how many in the battalion – maybe a hundred and there were a few nashos back at Terendak when we got there. Some of them were officers too – some became lieutenants.'

Darryl says there was always rivalry between the "regulars" and the "nashos." 'We'd call the lollies in Malaysia 'Nasho Pills' meaning that the nashos are soft. They used to say to us regulars that we joined the army to get a job, but they joined the army to do a job. That used to piss us off! My mate Bobby Taylor was a nasho. He used to skite about this National Service medal, and he'd wear it every time he fuckin' saw me. It used to give me the shits. Then the army turned around and gave a Regular Army medal so I would wear that and that gave him the shits.' He laughs, 'They were good blokes. Good soldiers too. I had a lot of good friends who were nashos and at the end of the day we were all fighting the same war.'

Like every introduction of a National Service Scheme since the early 1900s there was always opposition and 1965 was no different. Some might argue that objection to the fourth National Service Scheme was the most ferocious because it was fuelled by the objection to the Vietnam war that had begun to rise in the public. In 1965, a group of women formed the anti-conscription organisation,

Darryl 'Coop' Cooper

"Save our Sons". Established in Sydney but later formed in all states, this led to the "Save our Sons" protests across Australia.

Prior to their deployment, the next few weeks at Enoggera were jampacked with last minute training and preparation for Vietnam. There were lectures with officers and NCOs who had just come back from Vietnam. They would tell the soldiers about pansie pitts, mines and other things they encountered on their tours. The soldiers had medicals and needles. They had to learn how to speak some Vietnamese like 'stop', 'halt' and 'surrender'. There was more physical training, first aid courses and lectures. Darryl says, 'Our padres even gave us lectures on how to behave over there.'

During the weeks of preparation prior to deployment, the soldiers were given leave every night and on weekends. Darryl says, 'If we weren't on duty we would to go into Brisbane and drink at the Arcadia, the Treasury, the Lands Office and Lennons; they were the main pubs. We had a ball. Everyone in our platoon used to go in together. We had trams then from the city to Enoggera which was the last stop. You had to be twenty-one to drink then. We had an army ID on us, and they used to turn a blind eye. The barmaids used to look after us and if we didn't cause any trouble, they never worried…which we didn't back in those days.'

It was the 16th of May, and they only had a few days to go until they left for Vietnam. The men of 4th Platoon were all drinking at one of their local pubs. Darryl says, 'We were talking away and someone says, "How many more days have we got before we go to Vietnam?" Another bloke says, "We go on the 19th." I said, "What's the date today?" and he says, "The 16th of May." I said "Shit, I'm twenty-one today!"'

They celebrated Darryl's birthday into the night.

Darryl used to get a lot of 'lifts' back to the Enoggera Barracks with the military police. On the last night before boarding the *HMAS Sydney* they caught him again. He was in the main street of Brisbane and the MPs picked him up and took him back out to Enoggera to the guardhouse. The police at the guardhouse told Darryl to go back down to B Company… and so he did. When he got back to B Company the corporal told him to go to bed. He says, 'So I went down the lines, turned around and ran out the main gate, caught a taxi and beat the MPs back into town again. I got into a bloody fight in one of the cafes with a sailor. I should have stayed at the barracks.'

17
The Vung Tau Ferry

On the 19th of May 1967 the time had come for the soldiers of 2RAR to leave for their first tour in Vietnam. They assembled on the parade ground of the Enoggera Barracks, were given a boarding number which was placed in each soldier's slouch hat. They then boarded a convoy of army trucks which would take them to Hamilton Wharf on the Brisbane River preparing to board the troop carrier *HMAS Sydney*.

HMAS (Her Majesty's Australian Ship) *Sydney III* had many different roles since it had been launched in 1944. If the flight deck could talk, it would tell of its thousands of hours of service in the Royal Australian Navy lending its decks to pilot training. There'd be tales of deployment in the Korean War, of lending the runway to Sea Fury Fighters and Fireflies. Stories of sailing the oceans in extreme conditions and typhoons. It would boast 10,000 deck landings by 1953 before being maintained in reserve from 1958.

In 1962, both the Minister for Defence and the Prime Minister approved the Australian Army's proposal that the *Sydney* be taken out of reserve and reactivated as a fast troop transport carrier to be maintained at seven days' notice for sea.[xi] So, when in March, 1966

Beneath the Southern Cross I Stand

Harold Holt announced Australia would increase its commitment to Vietnam, the *HMAS Sydney* was to embark on her first voyage to Nui Dat carrying the troops of 5RAR and 6RAR. Between 1965 to 1972 the *HMAS Sydney* had a new job… from here on she would be known as the 'Vung Tau Ferry'.

In May 1967, Darryl and the other soldiers of 2RAR, loaded with all their gear and rifles boarded the *HMAS Sydney*.

They were sorted into their companies and allocated their mess decks. "Mess deck" is the navy term for living quarters or what the Army calls "barracks." The soldiers sorted out their sleeping arrangements, arranged their webbing and packs. They then made their way to the flight deck and as the band played military music the soldiers waved back to the crowd of family and friends watching on. There were mums, wives and girlfriends shedding tears for their men going to war. Dads, brothers, sisters and friends all watching on and as the band continued to play, the soldiers watched back from the flight deck.

The battalion was organised into three ranks and as the ship sailed into the Brisbane River the band played *Waltzing Matilda* and the Regimental Sergeant Major brought the soldiers to attention. They shouldered arms, gave a tremendous salute, and presented arms.

Darryl says, 'Little did we know that a living hell was awaiting us in Vietnam. Some of us would never see Australia again. Some would come back with horrific wounds; arms and legs missing. Some wouldn't come back at all.'

18
The Run to Vietnam

The *HMAS Sydney* sailed out of the Brisbane River and into Moreton Bay, setting course north up the Queensland Coast, past Redcliffe and the Sunshine Coast. Darryl recalls passing the coast, 'We could see the lights in the distance.'

It was the first afternoon on the ship and the men got their first navy beer ration: two cans of beer which they were pleased were the oversized cans that held 750ml each. They also received their first meal of the trip. There were so many men onboard that the meals were arranged into two sittings. Darryl explains, 'The ship was massive; it was a carrier. There might have been nine hundred soldiers on board plus the navy. When we boarded, we were issued with a red or blue tag which we hung with our dog tags around our neck. It would come over the loudspeaker, "Red or blue tags to the cafeteria now". I think the navy used to call it a cafeteria.'

When asked what a dog tag is Darryl explains, 'It is the nickname the soldiers gave to their ID discs. It tells the soldier's name, blood group, regimental number, nationality and religion. There are two tags worn around your neck; one the officer keeps to write letters back home and the other they put in your mouth when they bury you so when the war is over and they come to get you, they know who you are.' This is another reminder of the raw reality of the war they are about to enter.

After the soldiers eat, they go to their mess decks where they read books, play cards and where some would begin writing letters home. They are each given a book on basic Vietnamese and how their allied ranks looked. They then climb into their hammocks and go to sleep.

The next day the same again, "Red or blue tag to breakfast." After breakfast they take part in physical training and weapon skills. They would fire the weapons off the back of the ship. They undertake lessons about the ways and traditions of the Vietnamese people and how the VC (Viet Cong) would always wear black pyjamas. 'So, we were being taught that the Viet Cong wore these black pyjamas and when we got there ninety percent of the Vietnamese wore black pyjamas (that was their traditional dress). We thought the bloody place was overrun with Viet Cong…I think someone messed up there.'

Two days into the trip as they were steaming past Cairns, Darryl's platoon was to go on duty. Each platoon took a turn to do duties around the boat. One of which was to guard the trucks and helicopters on the flight deck. One night, Darryl and his mate, Johnny Barnes, who was also from 4RAR were tasked with flight deck guard between twelve midnight and two a.m. Darryl said to his mate, "Who in the bloody hell is going to steal this equipment in the middle of the Coral Sea?" So, they agreed for John to guard the first hour and Darryl to guard the second. Darryl would sleep out where the Bofor guns (anti-aircraft guns) used to be on the side of the boat before they were dismantled. Darryl resigns to his position for a sleep for the first hour of their duty.

Darryl 'Coop' Cooper

When the sergeant came up on the flight deck to check on the guards, he only found Barnsey up there and asked who was with him. Barnsey said, "Cooper and he is down in the cafeteria getting a cup of coffee." The sergeant leaned over the rail and again said to him "Who was that bloke who went to get a cup of coffee?" Barnsey said again, "Cooper." The Sergeant looked over and saw Darryl sleeping on the deck along the side of the ship. He yells out "Cooper!" Darryl was immediately charged for sleeping on duty.

The navy had a refuelling base on Manus Island. Darryl says, 'We were there refuelling and that's where I had to front up to this charge. I had to front the OC, Major Carter, but he referred me to the CO who was Lieutenant 'Chicka' Charlesworth, but he was already in Vietnam with the advanced party. So, I had to front the battalion 2IC Major Smith who we called the "angry Little Ant." He gave me a lecture about letting the battalion down and gave me seven days CB. I had to do any shitty jobs on the ship, had no time to myself and had to run around the flight deck every day for an hour. Let me tell you, running into a head wind on the flight deck of an aircraft carrier is no easy task, especially with all your gear and rifle. Some days my mate, Ian Atkinson, would run with me. When I got to Vietnam, I told everyone "I ran all the fuckin' way here."'

Vietnam was only another five or six days from Manus Island, Papua New Guinea via the South China Sea. Darryl was confined to barracks for the rest of the journey to Vietnam. 'After I fronted the "Angry Ant" and he gave me a lecture, the RSM Moon gave me a lecture as well. He said, "Cooper you're the luckiest man alive, the only way you'll die is to choke on a Kellogg's Cornflake early in the morning." Little did he know I would be shot in head a couple of months later.'

On the way over, the HMAS Sydney received a navy escort - the *HMAS Stuart*. 'Which was to protect us from enemy ships and submarines; it was a frigate. We decided to have a boxing competition against the two ships. I think there were about twelve bouts. The army won eleven and the other one was a draw. The sailors really did treat us well.'

When the *HMAS Sydney* sailed into Vietnamese waters, the *HMAS Stuart* came up beside their ship flying a massive flag saying, "Good Luck Black Drummers." With their horns going, all the sailors were out on deck giving 2RAR a salute wishing them all the best.

For the rest of the voyage, it was the same routine and then they reached Vung Tau Harbour. 'I will never forget that day. How gloomy it was, smoke coming out of the hills. Helicopters and jet fighters flying everywhere, artillery guns going off. We were on the flight deck with all our gear and rifles ready to go. Navy divers were sent down to check underneath the ship for any mines while the ship was in harbour. I could feel then that this was a fair dinkum war. I was just thinking back to a couple of days ago when the *HMAS Stuart* came up beside our ship flying the flag "Good Luck Black Drummers" and I was thinking we are going to need all the luck we could have.'

There is no more time to think as the sound from the helicopters on the flight deck drowns out their thoughts and the soldiers of 2RAR begin boarding. They are heading for their new home for the next twelve months. A place called Nui Dat in South Vietnam.

Darryl 'Coop' Cooper

19
1st Australian Task Force, Nui Dat

Loaded into Hui choppers on the flight deck of the HMAS Sydney, the destination is Nui Dat which was the headquarters of the First Australian Force (1ATF) in the province of Phuoc Tuy, South Vietnam.

'Flying over Vietnam we knew how the war was tearing people apart as we could see bomb craters all over the place.'

Nui Dat which means 'Dirt Hill' in Vietnamese was essentially just that, a hill that had been an old rubber plantation. It had its own airfield, Luscombe Airfield, which was built by the Royal Australian Engineers specifically for the 1st Australian Task Force. Opened in December 1966 this was a critical time for Australia's movement to carry out operations independently of the United States. To understand the importance of the Nui Dat base to Australia's commitment to Vietnam, it is important to understand a brief snapshot of how the base came about.

In April 1965 Prime Minister Robert Menzies announced the commitment of an Australian Battalion to Vietnam. 1st Battalion the Royal Australian Regiment (1RAR) was then deployed to Vietnam in June 1965. In the context of Darryl's timeline, you will recall that two years prior, when Darryl was in Infantry Training and about to be deployed to Malaysia, his platoon was drinking with 1RAR just before they were about to leave for Vietnam.

Upon arrival in Vietnam 1RAR essentially became a 3rd Battalion of the US 173rd Airborne Brigade based at Bien Hoa airfield. Between their arrival in June 1965 and their departure twelve months later in June 1966, 1RAR carried out a number of operations attached to the US Brigade.

It was at this time that Harold Holt had famously declared in one of his speeches 'All the way with LBJ'. It became apparent that there were significant differences in tactics between the two countries. The sheer size of the US army in both manpower and firepower allowed them to deploy quickly and thereby overwhelm the enemy successfully. As Darryl says, 'The Americans would come in guns blazing.' Conversely, the Australian army with far less manpower and fire support leaned to tactics of jungle warfare—search and destroy. In 1966 when 1RAR had left Vietnam for Australia, the Australian Government decided to replace the Battalion with a brigade-sized taskforce large enough to enable Australia to operate independently in Vietnam. The Phuoc Tuy Province was then allocated to the 1st Australian Task Force (1ATF).[xii]

5RAR and 6RAR were the first two battalions assigned to the taskforce and arrived in April and May 1966. At the same time Darryl had just arrived in Borneo, 5RAR and 6RAR had begun operations to secure the area around Nui Dat and build the base. Over the coming months, they undertook a number of patrolling and ambushing operations establishing the routine of one battalion protecting the base while the other undertakes operations off base. This is where on the 18th of August 1966 when Darryl was listening to the radio with his platoon in Borneo, he overheard how 6RAR were involved in the Battle of Long Tan. 6RAR were sent out from the Nui Dat base to locate the enemy and came into contact with Viet Cong. The battle resulted in a devastating seventeen killed and nineteen wounded.

Twelve months later 7RAR relieved 5RAR in Vietnam. Following them in May 1967, after touching down at Luscombe Airfield, Darryl and the other soldiers of 2RAR were loaded onto trucks to be transported to their new lines at Nui Dat.

2RAR were relieving 6RAR and as they were loading on the trucks, they crossed paths with 6RAR who were leaving Vietnam at the same time. 'They wished us all the luck because their D Company 6RAR had just been in the Battle of Long Tan. They reminded us that we had 364 days and a wakey to go.' A "wakey" is military slang for the last day before returning home.

It is important to note at this time New Zealand wanted to commit themselves to Vietnam, so they sent a rifle company and artillery battery that came under 2RAR's command.

20
2RAR Arrive at the Nui Dat Base

Entering through the "Pearly Gates" in a convoy of trucks the soldiers arrive at their base. 2RAR was on the left flank of the battalion.

The 2RAR battalion lines consisted of a number of prefabricated buildings which housed company headquarters, Q-Store, ORs mess, the boozer, the sergeant and officers' mess, the toilets and shower. Darryl says, 'We had toilets and showers and I was impressed.' Although, it was better than their living conditions in Borneo, it was far from five-star. The showers and latrines were surrounded by corrugated iron. They had hot water that was boiled on gas, and they would add some hot water to a bucket and string it up for their shower.

The rest of the base was a number of tents spread out. 'This was just the 2RAR base for all the frontline soldiers, the infantry like us, the SAS, engineers, artillery, ordnance, doctors and all that sort of stuff we need up the front. The other battalion bases were not far away.'

The tents were constructed in lines with sandbags built up to keep the rain out. Canvas was then thrown over the sandbags creating the walls of each tent. Duckboards were used as the floor of the tents as a small but important barrier between the soldiers and the ground. Each Section had three tents and there were four beds to a tent. 'The beds had mattresses which was better than Borneo where we had just a sleeping bag and stretcher. We also had pillows and within a couple of months we had sheets.' Darryl shared a tent with Ralph Hoger, Georgie Duff and the corporal of his Section (2), Brian 'Andy' Andrews.

In front of the tent lines were trenches with overhead protection in case they were attacked at base. 'The overhead protection was built in the side of the earth and was eighteen inches of head protection that you could sleep in and if an artillery or mortar round landed you were protected and never got hurt. We had our ammo and rations there and we could stay there for a couple of days if we needed to. We would use the trenches if we were attacked. We used them at "stand to" as well.'

Just beyond the trenches was barbed wire which surrounded the whole of Nui Dat and was the only protection between them and the Viet Cong. Within the barbed wire were Claymore mines. Distinguished by their three-word warning on the face of the mine "Front Toward Enemy", these mines were faced out from the wire. 'There were trackers or fire positions set up in the trenches where we could set the mines off so if the enemy did get in the wire, we had the mines as extra protection for the base.'

For the first week the soldiers were orientated around Nui Dat so they knew where everything was situated; Battalion Headquarters, Q-Store, Regimental Aid Post (RAP), Battalion Post Office, Transport Compound 'Everything we had to know and report to.'

21
The Horseshoe

About 8000 metres southeast of Nui Dat was a hill shaped like a horseshoe. Established as a permanent support base, the hill was used as a fire support base for field and medium artillery batteries which were in the range of troops operating in that area. 'So, we could go out further from Nui Dat and still have the protection of artillery.'

There was always one rifle company on duty at 'The Horseshoe' and each company would be there for six weeks at a time. Darryl's Company—B Company was second on the horseshoe. 'During the six weeks' occupation at Horseshoe we came under the direct command of the taskforce at Nui Dat. We were allotted artillery, mortars, engineers and some armoured support.'

The Horseshoe was chosen for its position as it dominated the approaches of the village of Dat Do—not far from Long Tan—and other villages along the Route 44. It supplied security for the village along that route from the Viet Cong.

It also had the job of protection of a twelve-kilometre minefield which was constructed by the engineers from the Horseshoe to the coast. The purpose of the minefield was to cut off the Viet Cong in eastern Phuoc Tuy from the Southern region and from the Viet Cong base in Long Hai Hills.[xiii]

The minefield was not successful, and in fact, Darryl says, 'The Viet Cong were coming in at night-time, pinching the mines from the minefield and laying them on tracks that we walk on and blowing us up. The army had to clear the mines so what the army did, they had this tank with all these chains. They would drive through the minefield with these chains whipping across in front of them exploding all the mines so the VC couldn't use them.'

22
Back to Basics at the Base

For the first couple of weeks, the soldiers had to climatise to the tropical weather of Vietnam—the heat and humidity was unbearable.

Making life more uncomfortable was when the rainy season came bringing monsoons, insects and mosquitos. Known for its reputation of malaria, the soldiers had to take malaria pills twice a day. The sergeant would have a 'Malaria Parade' in the morning and again at night. 'He would call your name out. He would give you the pill. You would take it in front of him and he would then mark the roll book that you had taken your pill. Then that night there was another parade where you would take your pill again and he would mark the roll book. At that stage it was six p.m. and we had to roll our sleeves down to protect us from mosquitos at night.'

They continued the army routine of physical fitness and weapons training, and undertook talks in their section, platoon and company, of tactics under fire. They also had to undertake TAOR patrols which is Tactical Area of Responsibility outside the wire. 'We would go out on patrol to make sure there was no suspicious activities going on like VC digging tunnels under Nui Dat or setting up mortar bases so they could fire at Nui Dat.'

Darryl 'Coop' Cooper

Darryl says, 'The boozer would open at 16:00 hours and if you were not on duty, you could go and have a couple of beers. We did not have to sign for two beers like in Borneo; we drank until the company allocation ran out. Like Borneo, we were not allowed glass in the boozer. I guess the officers were afraid we would cut ourselves—again don't worry that we are in a warzone. The officers and sergeants were allowed beer and spirits.'

The soldiers were paid with American Military Payment Certificates (MPC). A can of soft drink was ten cents, a beer was fifteen cents, a packet of cigarettes was fifteen cents. 'It was all paper money, we had five cent notes, ten cent notes. If you went to the American PX you could by radiograms, records, cameras and all that with your MPC. There were no dollars whatsoever—I think they were trying to prevent the black market.'

Darryl says of the early days in Nui Dat, 'You'd look up into the sky and there would be three phantom jets flying over. Sometimes in the morning you would look up and see vapour trails and see B52 bombers on their way to North Vietnam to bomb targets up there. Otherwise, the days became very normal at Nui Dat as we got to know each other very well and respected each other.

We had arrived at Nui Dat on the 30th of May 1967. What a journey it was just to get there. We had all looked around at each other and wondered who would make it back to Australia. We all hoped we would make it back, but it was up to each of us to look after each other.

We were due to go out on our first operation on the 4th of June and as I laid in my bed that night I was thinking—as I'm sure every soldier was—how would I react under fire? Because in Malaysia and Borneo there was no angry shot fired at me and I had not fired an angry shot. I was hoping I would not run, would not be too scared to fight back, freeze and would not be able to protect any of my mates. I was soon to find out very, very shortly what being fired at was like.'

Part 4

1st Tour Vietnam, The Operations

As the storm gets closer, you hear a gentle rumble of thunder in the distance. The sheep and cattle begin to find shelter in the fields. You put your hand out palm to the sky and feel the slight drops of rain like pins and needles on your skin. The sky is suddenly illuminated with lightning. The first crack of thunder jolts you. The wind picks up. The trees move with force. The door to the shed bangs. The windmill clicks faster. More lightning. More thunder. Banging. Clicking. More lightning. More thunder. Until the sky lets go in a heavy downpour. You tuck your head and shoulders down to protect yourself from the stinging rain against your face. It is a downpour so loud and consuming you can't hear anything else...

NB. Darryl has sourced some of the details of the operations: locations, phases and dates from the ANZAC Battalion in South Vietnam 1967-68 Volume 1 which covers in detail all fifteen operations undertaken by 2RAR during 1967-68.

23
A Day at Barossa

When the soldiers were moving around Nui Dat, they had to have their weapons with them at all times. It must be within one metre and if not, they would be charged on the spot. They were issued with new ammunition for their rifles, machine guns and M16s. They were also issued with grenades, Claymore mines, plastic explosives and spare batteries for the platoon sig set. They would take as much ammunition as they could carry and still carry out their activities. 'We were allowed this because D Company 6 RAR ran out of ammunition at the Battle of Long Tan. Most of them were sitting with their backs to the trees with their machetes out waiting for the final attack.'

The men would also carry at least four water bottles and five days' rations depending on where they were operating. It was generally mixed up with three American rations and two Australian. Darryl says, 'American rations were too rich—they had cream instead of milk and everything was sweet.'

Darryl was now ready to go out on his first operation—Operation Barossa. The order was given to move out. They mounted trucks and were driven to Luscombe Airfield where they boarded assault heavy Hui helicopters and flew to Binh Ba airstrip which is not far from Nui Dat (fifteen to twenty kilometres east of Nui Dat). The purpose of Darryl's first operation was for the soldiers of the Australian Army to get used to working with the Americans, boarding and disembarking the helicopters fully loaded with all the gear they had to carry.

They also had to get used to the tactics of 2RAR. 'A lot of us were 4RAR blokes and we had to get used to their tactics—each battalion's tactics are different. We had to learn to constantly look out for mines. Also, we didn't travel on tracks—we'd go through the bush.'

They were flown back to Nui Dat the same day.

24
Overnight in Darwin

The next operation was an overnight op. They loaded up with all the extra gear the needed: sleeping gear, rations, dixies, cutlery, cigarettes and anything else they needed to be able to stay out for days at a time and to be able to move great distances.

On this op, the soldiers were choppered out about eleven kilometres east of the base. 'Our company did come across an old VC camp which had not been in use for some time. We found a lot of ox cart tracks which the VC used to transport most of their equipment around. We still had not had any contact with the enemy whatsoever.'

They returned to the base the next afternoon, cleaned their weapons, attended the malaria parade, showered, rolled their sleeves down, and then headed to the boozer.

25
The Long Green

The next operation—Operation Geraldton lasted five or six days. They were to patrol east of Dat Do—an area which was called The Long Green. The enemy had been known to use this area for equipment and arms.

Several successful operations were conducted by 6RAR and 7RAR but the enemy was still persistent in the use of the area. B Company went in on assault helicopters into the landing zone, Dee Why, which had been secured by A company and battalion headquarters. Two sections of the Mortars now move alongside Armoured Personnel Carriers (APC) and C Company moved to the landing zone, Balmoral. Darryl's company and D Company swept to the north to a blockade position to stop any enemy movements to the north.

A Company was the only company to have contact with the Viet Cong. They had wounded and captured a VC who later died of his wounds.[xiv]

'During that operation we had four blokes wounded, one VC killed, 160 pounds of TNT and a number of grenades destroyed, 150 pounds of salt, six and a half tonnes of rice, and we destroyed ninety bunkers, 200 weapon pits and as well as a large area of tunnels.'

Then it was back to Nui Dat to clean their weapons, receive ammunition, enter the showers, malaria pill parade, sleeves down and into the boozer.

A short break in this cycle, 2RAR started up a beach party. Each section was to go to the beach at Vung Tau and spend a day there. The Australian army had built a club down there with accommodation. It was named after Peter Badcoe who had won a Victoria Cross in Vietnam. 'Peter Badcoe was one of the blokes we buried in Malaysia. He is still buried at Terendak Garrison.'

Darryl recalls, 'The first beach party did not go too well because the boys got pissed in Vung Tau and took on the American and Australian military police. So, the beach parties got cancelled after that. It was one particular section that fucked it all up and to this day we have never let them live it down. So once again I missed out.'

26
Sitting Ducks

The next operation was Paddington and the Australian Army would be working with the American Army. The Australian Army was made up of 2RAR, 7RAR, A Squadron 3rd Cavalry Regiment, 4th Field Artillery Regiment, 1St field squadron of Engineers, 161 independent "recce"—reconnaissance—flight RAAF. Joined with the American Army, this was the biggest operation Darryl would be involved in so far.

The area they were going into was north-north east of Xuyen Moc. 'It was known to be a stronghold of the enemy—the 275 Regiment belonging to the North Vietnamese Army (NVA) 5th Division. There were also rumours of 274 Regiment NVA hanging around the area at the time which would have been hundreds of enemy. We thought we would be in the middle of this.'

The first phase started with the Army of the Republic of South Vietnam (ARVN) moving into a diversionary operation north-west of the area.

Phase 2 was to concentrate on this area of operation.

Phase 3 – after all the forces were in position, the 11th Army Cavalry Regiment of the United States (11ACR) went north on Route

Darryl 'Coop' Cooper

329. This was only an overgrown jungle trail. Two battalions of Vietnamese marines were operating in the north at the same time. 2RAR was to carry out an air assault on a landing zone called Bob and 7RAR was to attack north on Xuyen Moc towards 2RAR.

Phase 4 – once the 11th Cavalry Regiment had linked up with the Vietnamese marines, they were to sweep south-east. 2RAR and 7RAR were to commence patrolling to locate and destroy all Viet Cong buildings and caches.

Phase 5 – while the forces were both carrying out these orders the engineers were to clear along both sides of Route 23 from Dat Do to Xuyen Moc so the VC could not ambush along that route.

The operation begins and B Company, 2RAR was moved to Xuyen Moc airstrip where they mounted assault helicopters to land at the landing zone, Bob. The high commander was worried they would be wiped out so before this assault, the area around the airstrip was heavily bombarded with medium and heavy artillery for five to ten minutes. [xv] Darryl says, 'There were phantom jets dropping napalm, rockets and bombs, naval guns firing on ships out on the South China Sea and the gunship helicopters with their rockets and machineguns.'

'While we were going in, the machineguns on the helicopters were spraying the tree line just beyond the paddy fields where we were about to land. As we jumped out of the helicopters, we were firing our weapons too. But the paddy fields were wet, and we got stuck in the mud up to our knees. Some up to their waist. We were like sitting ducks in the middle of a paddy field. We soon made it to the tree line. Thank Christ! We found out later that there was one Viet Cong there and he got away. The way we came in, I reckon he would have run to Hanoi and been there within the hour.'

B Company stayed in this position for a few days. On this operation they could not drink the water because of the Napalm. They would get their water from the rain and had a couple of hoochies pinned out to catch the water. This went on for about three or four days. They were patrolling the area, destroying Viet Cong camps, bunkers, weapon pits and tunnels.

They then moved back to the landing zone Bob and choppered out along Route 23 to protect the roads so that the Americans and South Vietnamese Army could draw back to their bases.

'At the end of our operation, our losses were one Australian, one Australian wounded and three APCs destroyed. Enemy losses were forty killed.'

This was 2RARs biggest operation yet. 'We're talking about 2000 Australian infantry troops joined with the American Army.' The Australian Army was following the tactics of the Americans and Darryl says, 'They went in guns blazing. It would have cost a fortune in wasted ammo. That's the difference between and us and the Americans—if it was up to us, we would have snuck into the area on foot, found the enemy—in this instance that 1 VC bloke—and then shoot. This shows you why the Australians wanted their own province.'

'They flew us back to Nui Dat. If I remember right, I think we got a rum ration that night.'

27
The Burden

If they were not on duty their free time was spent playing sport: rugby league, cricket or volleyball. 'We would have to pick out an area where there were no star pickets or wire and trenches, but where there was a will there was a way. One of our mates, Dave Whitehouse, would commentate our rugby games on a tape recorder and play it at the boozer that night. Just like when we were kids, we had to make our own fun. He would say things like, "Cooper's now got the ball and he's got to get around such and such, but you'd need a cut lunch and fuckin' water bottle to get around him!" Or he'd say, "What's his name just went down that trench, get him back off the wire, he's still in play!" Then he'd go over to an ad and he'd say, "Just switching over to Wimbledon now." Or he'd go over to the news, and he hated old Arthur Caldwell, who was the leader of the opposition at the time, and he'd put shit on him all day!'

Darryl laughs, 'In the end the Lieutenant said I had to stop them because there were too many blokes getting hurt. So, we didn't have enough blokes to go out on patrol with. He said, "Cooper, you better stop this fuckin' rugby. You can have volleyball and cricket but no rugby league!"'

Beneath the Southern Cross I Stand

Being back at Nui Dat was not without incident. One night the soldiers were down at the boozer. It was monsoon season, and the weather was wild. Suddenly one of the M60s opened up. They all hurried back to their trenches and started firing their weapons. The men in the gun pit thought there was VC on the wire, so they started firing. The next morning a clearing patrol was sent out and found no trace of enemy movements and no major tunnels were found. What had happened was a branch broke off one of the rubber trees, fell across the trip wire and the trip flare went off. The men on the guns thought the enemy was there and started firing.

Darryl recalls, 'Major Carter our OC was not impressed and told the company on parade how he felt. Then as we were lining up for breakfast that morning, it came over the armed forces radio that the Australian Base was attacked last night at Nui Dat but the enemy was repelled. What it was; was the fuckin' rubber branch.'

The next operation was Operation Cairns.

Darryl says, 'We had been in Vietnam a couple of months now and had fired the odd angry shot and heard them fire back at us. In contact or in action I would lie there and hear the crack of bullets go over my head which was good because if you could hear the crack, it did not hit you. When the artillery mortars and rockets hit your position, you would grind your teeth, wait a few seconds and if you felt no pain, you were right. You would hear the explosion a few seconds later.'

The next op was to be conducted at the Long Green again which remained a VC hot spot. Agent reports were that there had been an increase of VC movement in the area since their last operation there. 2RAR were to search and destroy in the area and to patrol and ambush the tracks and clearings.[xvi]

The operation would go for six days and Darryl's platoon were in an ambush position on one clearing for three days. They positioned themselves right on the edge of the tree line watching the track that

Darryl 'Coop' Cooper

came up to the tree line. They were at fifty percent stand to which meant one man was on duty and the other was resting. Those on duty were at "stand to", stomach to the ground, weapon in hand, watching the track just beyond the tree line where they lay. On this day, the platoon commander told them to swap their positions so they could talk in different positions. They left their machineguns where they were and swapped positions.

Darryl was resting beside the machinegun when the other soldier that was with him tapped him on the shoulder and said very quietly, "ARVN." Darryl says 'They were not ARVN—they were the VC. I counted about three or four through first because I was on the left flank, I wasn't going to get the first one. They would walk on inside our ambush.

Then I opened up with my M60 and fired two rounds and the gun jammed. I looked up at this VC who was about two paces from me. He was bringing his AK47 around to shoot me in the back as I was trying to unjam the gun. His eyes…he was shitting himself as much as I was. All I can remember is his eyes. Boy, was I waiting for that pain but then the rest of the platoon opened up and the VC fled into the tree line across the clearing and out of sight.'

Darryl was starting to learn his reaction under fire. His questions while lying in bed the night before the first operation: Would I run? Would I freeze? Would I be able to protect my mates? These questions were now all being answered.

He says, 'You are in the middle of a contact, and you are only thinking of saving your mates and saving yourself and you do these things, and you don't remember them until after. Like when you are standing to and waiting for a counter attack. Later you are thinking why the hell did I do that? I should have run away. But you don't think it through, it just comes automatic to you.'

That night in the silence of the jungle of Vietnam, they could hear the VC firing their AK47s into the air. 'They were signalling each other to join up again. You would hear a bang and then half an hour later you would hear another bang.'

After that contact, they were on the move again. B Company had no contact with the enemy again during Operation Cairns. D Company, however, had a number of incidents. 'One of the soldiers of D Company stood on a mine which injured three soldiers. Then, when they had moved on, they found a well-constructed VC Camp. On the edge of that camp another soldier detonated a mine which killed two of his mates.'

They were choppered back to Nui Dat, cleaned their weapons, attended the malaria parade, showered, rolled their sleeves down then headed to the boozer. The feeling of this nightly ritual for 2RAR was beginning to change. The heavy cloud of what was happening was beginning to descend and the burden they would carry for the rest of their lives had now attached itself to the men.

Darryl says, 'Now our soldiers—D Company—are getting killed on mines. We are starting to really feel what's going on and that we are in a warzone. At the boozer the night after Cairns, the feeling was there, not many people were talking that much. A lot of them had gone through Corp and rookie training with these blokes and some of them came from the same small town… they knew their sisters and mothers. One of the blokes was drinking in the boozer with me just a few nights before. We had lost a few mates that day and things started to change after that.'

28
Operation Atherton

Back at Nui Dat the soldiers were back to tasks at base: replacing sandbags, raking leaves, generally keeping their lines in good condition. The officers would inspect their tents looking for any illegal items, such as captured weapons or ammunition and particularly alcohol which some of the men used to get sent over from Australia or bring back from leave.

Each soldier would get ten days off a year; five days 'R and C' which is "Rest in Country". They would go to Vung Tau which had a lot of bars, a swimming pool at the Peter Badcoe club, and also a beach where they could swim. It was a good break from Nui Dat. There was also five days for 'R and R'—Rest and Recuperation. They could go to Singapore, Bangkok, Tokyo, Thaipei and there was talk that the government was going to open up Australia for R and R for the Americans. Darryl says, 'I missed out on my trip to Bangkok—I had five days to go when it happened.'

It was time to go out again. This time it was on Operation Atherton. The battalion was to go north on Route 23 and west of Song Rai to patrol, search and destroy. 7RAR was conducting similar patrols to the west and it would also include searching the villages of

Beneath the Southern Cross I Stand

Dat Do and Lang Phuo Hai. Elections were to be held at the end of this operation on the 3rd of September 1967. The VC were trying to stop the villagers from getting to the polling booths.

On the 19th of August, C Company was deployed again by RAAF choppers to a landing zone which had been secured by A Company. Two days later, B Company was given the task of protecting engineers who were clearing mines from Route 23 and at the same time secure the landing zone for Delta Company to fly in. During this period the Americans had ordered in a B52 strike conducted in the jungle south of Route 23.[xvii] Darryl says, 'While all this was going on, we had been in contact with the enemy several times. All you could hear and see as the B52 strike was going on was big flashes of red and yellow and the ground shook beneath you.'

The next day the battalion concentrated along Route 23 for the search of Dac Dao. 2RAR concentrated on searching the eastern part of the village, while 7RAR concentrated on the west part of the village.

Darryl says, 'No attempt was made to cordon off the village. All we were looking for in each house were tunnels, food hides, propaganda material, VC or wanted persons. The Americans would use voice aircraft—they would fix aircraft with loud speakers and were capable of releasing leaflets to the villages.'

When asked how the villagers reacted to the searches, Darryl recalls, 'The villagers were told to stay in their houses until the search was completed. They knew they had to do it. They didn't like it…you would be weary if soldiers were coming into your house. They looked upon you and well, we didn't know who was friend or who was foe. Their own Vietnamese army and police used to treat them badly and they weren't sure how we would treat them. We were respectful and they were a bit surprised.'

The next day the battalion was moved by helicopters to the second concentration area east of the village of Lang Phuo Hai which

Darryl 'Coop' Cooper

was to be searched the same as Dac Dao. During the day another B52 strike was put in on the eastern side of the village.

'Since we were at the coast, everyone took their uniform off and went for a swim in the sea. It must have been a sight to see 500 nude Australians on the beach. This day was marred when a private of D Company stood on a bloody mine and was killed.'

The villages were divided between 2RAR and 7RAR. No significant finds were made except for a few draft dodgers who were turned over to the South Vietnamese authorities. They carried on patrolling and having contacts with the enemy and returned to Nui Dat on the 3rd of September 1967.

'Boy, we had done a lot of hard work on that operation. Then it was back to clean our weapons, malaria parade, shower, roll down our sleeves and go to the boozer.'

'During Atherton there would have been a couple of blokes wounded and some enemy killed. We had a lot of contacts and sometimes you get no results. Some I can remember and don't want to and some I can't remember. By now we were seeing some horrible things going on...not by us but what the Viet Cong did to the villagers. We were in a village one day and this girl was screaming and screaming, and she was having a baby and the Viet Cong were there and they wouldn't let anyone in. When the VC saw us coming, they fled and then we sent a section in after them. We killed one of them and the other got away because they know their way around the jungle. It was at that time the village midwife came along to help the girl that was screaming, and we also had one of our medics go in there. Five or ten minutes later we heard this baby cry and it was a little boy.'

There were other stories of cruelty that didn't end so well. The VC crimes against the villagers were horrendous. 'We—the soldiers—gotta do something about that you know. But it's too horrific to tell some of those stories of what the VC were doing. People shouldn't live with that…only us.'

29
Slope 30

2RAR was now appointed a new Lieutenant, Lieutenant First Class Jim Connolly who was transferred from Assistant Adjutant of Battalion Headquarters to 4th Platoon. Lieutenant McTaggart was to replace him as Assistant Adjutant, so it was a clean swap.

After Atherton, Darryl was sent on a five-day Rest in Country to Vung Tau. 'I thought this would be a real break from Nui Dat. At the same time, a Sergeant from 5 Platoon was also sent for his R in C; his name was Tom Birnie and we got on well together. I didn't know about an incident that had happened back at 4th Platoon when our Sergeant Jack Woods was transferred from 4 Platoon to 5 Platoon so when we got back to Nui Dat, Sergeant Birnie was our new platoon sergeant. We became good friends over the years.'

The next operation was Ainslie. B Company did not get deployed on this operation because they were to occupy the Horseshoe for six weeks. This operation was a taskforce for resettlement, search and destroy. It was to be conducted north of Nui Dat on Route 2 in the area of Xa Bang, which was in Phuoc Tuy province.

They were supported by the usual units; A Squadron, 3rd Cavalry Regiment, 4th Field Regiment, 183rd Artillery A battery. The 2nd of the 35th Engineers 1st Field Squadron, 1SAS, 1AR (Australian Reinforcement) unit, 161 independent recce (reconnaissance) flight RAAF.

The VC area around Xa Bang was known as slope 30 which was a key centre for supplies for the VC 5th division. The supplies: clothing, medical, wire, telephone equipment, cables, rice and other general supplies were moved from Saigon along Route 2 north of Nui Dat which was the area of Long Khanh.

The forces that they were expected to have contact with during this operation were elements of the 274 and 275 Regiment of the North Vietnamese Army, D445 Provisional Battalion —local VC guerrilla groups.

The Viet Cong moved the supplies from the centres at slope 30 to the VC units in the jungles. The purpose of Operation Ainslie was to close down the VC operation on slope 30 and thereby restrict the movement of supplies to all their units in the jungle.

The operation was to be conducted in four phases. A new hamlet 'Ap Sauri Nghe' would be constructed north of Nui Dat for the families who lived on slope 30. The taskforce would conduct a census of the families. A fire support base would be established south of Ap Ngai Gia. Once the villagers were moved to their new home, the engineers would destroy the farms and houses in the area and declare two hundred metres each side of Route 2 thereby forcing the VC out of the area. The final phase was moving the First Australian Task Force by APC and helicopters back to Nui Dat.

While the operation was being conducted, the 11th Army Cavalry Regiment which was the American force was to carry out similar tasks along Route 2.

2RAR was to operate in the south and 7RAR was to operate in the north. B Company was in occupation of the Horseshoe.[xviii]

Darryl 'Coop' Cooper

'The resettlement was accomplished very successfully with the villagers receiving their new plots of land and homes. During this period the battalion had a lot of contacts with the enemy. By now, 2RAR was a good and ready combat battalion,' Darryl says, 'I suppose the boys had a lot of conversations in the boozer when they returned to Nui Dat.'

B Company back at the Horseshoe were having a more relaxing period. Darryl says, 'We still had work to do. We lived in bunkers just like Borneo and had slit trenches from one bunker to another. We had to maintain our bunkers and slit trenches by replacing any damaged sandbags.'

One of the duties at Horseshoe was to man two checkpoints at Dac Do village—one to the north and one to the south. Three to four men would man the checkpoint to check the villager's work permits when they left the village and again upon their return. There was a curfew from 1800 hours to 0600 hours in the morning.

The other main duty at Horseshoe was to man the artillery guns. As explained earlier, Horseshoe was a fire support base to support the infantry if they got too far out from Nui Dat.

Darryl says, 'We also had a mess there where we could get fresh rations and had a beer ration at night. One of our diggers who was a baker from Jerilderie used to cook for us, Geoff Pitt. I remember some of the nights at the Horseshoe we would have what we call a yippee shoot where we would fire off our old ammunition. We would light the sky up, especially with tracers flying through the air. There were nights we would watch a B52 strike to our north. We would again see the sky light up…hear a big rumble and the ground would shake. I pity those enemies being in the middle of it.'

B Company moved off the Horseshoe early, around the 29th of September, to participate in Operation Kenmore. 'Sadly, the Viet Cong found out we were leaving the Horseshoe and the next morning they ambushed the new checkpoint diggers and killed and wounded the diggers. Actually, it was our turn—B Company—to be at the checkpoint that morning but we were moved off the Horseshoe early. One of my mates from 4RAR and from Rockhampton, Stewie Harold, was killed at the checkpoint that day.'

In one of those serendipitous moments that seemed to happen to Darryl quite often, he explains, 'A year later, on Anzac Day in Rockhampton I was drinking with a bloke all day and then he broke my heart when he told me Stewie had been his son.'

30
Ho Tram Cape

The next Operation—Kenmore was a search and destroy operation in the Ho Tram Cape area in the south east of the Phuc Tuy province. 2RAR had all of the usual support units including 7RAR. This was an important VC area and had been known for the past twelve months as the beaches of the cape had been used by the VC to resupply by sea. They had learned this from captured VC and other agents in the area. The enemy were mainly cells of the VC resupply units. These cells were fostered by the Vietnamese family who fed them and made Ho Chi Minh clothing and other equipment needed by the VC. The members came from north Vietnam and many of them were killed by 7RAR. [xix]

B Company was now off the Horseshoe and was moved by APCs to the Cape to secure the area. C Company took their position on the Horseshoe. D Company remained at Nui Dat to protect the new hamlet. Darryl recalls, 'We also had to fly in 106 field batteries via Xuyen Moc to cover our position and this move was carried out without incident.'

2RAR Companies moved forward and commenced the sweep northward. 7RAR commenced operations to the east and as the companies moved north, they came across a number of VC camps. They discovered that the camps had been evacuated. Darryl says, 'These camps were covered in bunker systems, and they were also booby trapped...thank Christ D Company wasn't there!'

On the 3rd and 4th of October V Company and A Company had contact with the VC; killed four and wounded one. They had received intelligence that the VC were constructing a fortified village in the area. A Company went south to search the eastern zone and Victor Company moved to the western edge. B Company was sent to search an area in the jungle north west. [xix]

'I think it was during this operation that our company was leading the battalion and our platoon was leading the company. A message came down from company headquarters that a K1W1 (Kiwi) Company was near our area and to look out for them. Bob Murray's section was up front with their Scout Jacko leading. He had received the message. He came across past the bend in the track and there was someone there and Jacko waved thinking it was a K1W1 and the bloke waved back and then each looked down and saw the weapons each man was carrying. He had an AK47 and Jacko had an Owen Gun. It was the VC. They both opened up. Jacko wounded the VC but he fled and left a blood trail so our OC called in the trackers with their dogs. The blood trail led into the Song Rai. The dogs could not track anything in the water and the search was called off.'

B Company's search of the area proved futile, however, Jacko's error and wave to the VC did serve a purpose. Darryl explains, 'The Owen gun was an Australian weapon used in the Second World War, Korea, Malaya, Malaysia and Borneo. Its calibre was a 9mm with a very low trajectory and having only 9mm ammo—which was also used in the 9mm pistols that the officers used to carry—you could nearly see the projectile leave the barrel and we reckon they used to ricochet off the leaves in the jungle. So, after that all scouts carried an M16 ArmaLite Automatic Rifle.'

Darryl 'Coop' Cooper

Then it was the usual, back to Nui Dat to clean weapons, shower, malaria parade, boozer.

31

Sante Fe

26 October to 19 November, 1967

Operation Sante Fe was to be a Taskforce operation to be conducted with the close co-operation of the 9th American Division and the 18th Division of the Vietnamese Army. The aim was to destroy elements of the 5th VC Division who were operating in the North-East of Phuoc Tuy Province known as the May Tao Secret Zone.

This operation was to be conducted over three weeks between October and November 1967. The area the task force was to operate in was important to the VC for bases, food production, communication routes and staging areas. Darryl explains, 'A staging area is where they can assemble a body of troops to get ready for an attack or to move into another area. This area had been searched before but not in detail as our taskforce were about to do.'

The first taskforce struck towards Thun Tich and about ten kilometres beyond the American 9th Division would attack from the north-west and elements of the 18th Vietnamese Division would strike from the north. Special long-range patrols were to operate on the eastern flank. As far as the taskforce was concerned the operations would occur in three phases between the 26th and 31st of October.ˣˣ

Darryl says, 'There were a few smaller contacts with the enemy but no big battles so far. We crossed our fingers that it would stay like this as we were expecting more contact in this area.'

'On the 4th of November, several contacts were made. A Company captured prisoners and B Company, killed one and wounded two others and captured one.'

'From the 6th to the 8th of November, the Company had no contacts with the enemy but had found a large number of bunkers, buildings, tunnels and equipment; sewing machines and bicycles to arms and ammunition. 2RAR had pushed to the north sweep and then moved to the south towards Xuyen Moc.'

'On the 9th of November during a contact with the VC, C Company had two of their soldiers wounded during the operation.'

Darryl says, 'At this time, the operations were now getting longer. We were resupplied with water, rations and ammunition every five days. We also got issued with an SP pack by the Americans which contained cigars, cigarettes, chewing tobacco, chocolate, lollies, toothpaste and chewing gum. I don't think our officers were too happy with all the shit they gave us. I think that would have made our colonel's hair stand on end if were smoking cigars.

We never showered. We never took our boots off. So, the enemy could smell us a mile away and fled out of the operation area. When we first used to go out on ops, you used to hoochy up with your mate…you know put our tents up. You could clip them together and make a two-man tent. Now getting towards the end of each operation, your mate would be hoochied over here and you'd be hoochie over there because you used to stink that much.

The only time we washed was when we crossed the Song Rai. I don't know how they used to do it, but every time we would cross a river or a creek it would be just before we hoochied up, so we'd have wet fuckin' socks and boots all night.'

For the remainder of Operation Sante Fe no further contacts with the enemy were made although the companies continued to find camps and installations.

On the 17th of November, 2RAR returned to Nui Dat by the 135th Helicopter Company. B Company moved to a fire support base to relieve a Company of 7RAR and A Squadron 3rd Cavalry Regiment (Aus). For the protection of the artillery battery, B Company remained there with the 108 Field Battery which was deployed to Xuyen Moc to cover the final withdrawal back to Nui Dat.

Darryl says, 'The operation was an overwhelming success and the VC as far as we were concerned were out of our area.'

Back at Nui Dat, they cleaned their weapons, attended the malaria parade, showered, rolled their sleeves down then headed to the boozer.

2RAR had been in Vietnam for six months now and the operations were getting longer. Darryl says, 'Most of the operations we had cleared the VC out of the area that we operated in, but after time they filtered back. Our army wasn't big enough to stay there.

We had also learnt the VC tactics by now which was to hit us and run away. They weren't soldiers, they were guerrillas. That's why you will find during these early operations we didn't have too many killed or wounded or many enemy killed. The tactics of the Viet Cong was to upset us, to attack us and run. The job of the VC was to help supply the North Vietnamese Army that was coming down and to terrorise the villagers to get them on their side.'

'What made it worse was that the South Vietnamese were doing the same thing. Instead of doing what we were doing which was resettling them and giving them land, money and looking after them. That's what the villagers appreciated more. Even though people didn't know back home what was going on...they reckon we were killing babies and this sort of shit. But as I said at the RSL that's what we went to South Vietnam for...so they could express their opinion. The people in Australia can express their opinion and are free to say what they like. Me...I was proud of what we were doing in Vietnam to help the villagers.'

32

Can't See the Forest…

23rd November to 5th January

In early December the rice harvest was beginning, and the enemy would try to procure most of the harvest for their units. They would do this via a number of methods. The VC local contacts would buy small amounts of rice that they would take to pick up points to be stored and later collected by the VC.

Sometimes the VC would disguise themselves as policemen to pass through the village checkpoints.

Finally, the VC used armed parties to visit farms and collect paddy taxes where husking took place in the fields. This was a very common practice in the Phuoc Tuy Province. [xxi]

Darryl says, '2RAR and 7RAR were allotted zones where these VC harvest activities were carried out. We were to patrol, ambush and deny the VC the opportunity to obtain the rice and taxes. 2RAR were allotted an area north and south of Route 23, east of Dat Do and Nui Dat and the northern zone of the village Binh Gia. Victor Company maintained company and platoon patrols throughout

Darryl 'Coop' Cooper

November to January. The company had no successful contacts with the enemy during this period.'

In the eastern area of the Long Green D Company and then B Company were active from the 25th of November to the 18th of December. In an attempt to deceive the VC, B Company were settled in the area on the same helicopters that brought D Company out. In this zone, D Company had killed 5 VC and B Company had killed two.

A and C Company were active between the 23rd of November and the 14th of December North of Route 23. Again, in an attempt to deceive the VC they left a constant group of A company and C Company behind while the bulk of the company were flown back to Nui Dat. In this period, A and C Company came into contact with a number of VC and they had killed and wounded some of them. Unfortunately, on the 27th of November a patrol of A Company detonated a booby trap while searching a camp. The explosion killed one soldier and wounded another. Again, on the 30th of November, A Company were on patrol examining a track and a mine was command detonated killing two soldiers and wounding eight.

From the 14th to 31st of December, C and D Company maintained patrols in this area. There were no contacts with the enemy at this time. ^{xxii}

The final phase was conducted by A and B Company in the northern area between the 2nd and 5th of January. This was quite unique as Darryl explains, 'B Company operated outside of the range of the field guns so we had no protection. I didn't know that at the time or I would have been fuckin' shitting myself.'

The battalion also maintained TAOR (Tactical Area of Operational Responsibility) patrols around Nui Dat and patrols looking after the new hamlet Ap Soui Nghe and around the hills of the Nui Dinh mountains. Darryl says, 'We were kept pretty bloody busy.'

Beneath the Southern Cross I Stand

2RAR also carried out a search of the village of Hoi My and Ngai Giao. The Vietnamese authorities carried out searches of Dat Do, Xa An Nhgot, Xa Ng Dien. This operation denied the VC access to the rice harvest in this area. Darryl says, 'While we were searching all of the villages the VC couldn't get to the rice.'

There were a few smaller operations that took place in the middle of Operation Forest.

Operation Canungra 3rd and 4th of December.

A search and destroy operation, the Battalion was to cordon off the village of Xa Hoi My situated on Route 44 south of Nui Dat. Darryl says, 'Through intelligence they had found out the villagers were neutral to slightly hostile towards the allies. They knew that VC relatives and sympathisers lived in the area and that some guerrillas depended on the village for support in the form of clothing, food and information. The village was also completely surrounded by rice paddies of which the villagers relied on for their livelihood. There were sixty-two known buildings, an old Vietnamese Army post and the ruins of a French Forte in the village. During this operation A, C and D Company remained on Operation Forest.'

The plan was for Victor Company and the Anti-Tank Platoon to be moved by helicopter from the Horseshoe and Nui Dat.

Darryl explains, 'Although in Vietnam the Anti-Tank Platoon became Trackers because the Viet Cong didn't have tanks. Our Anti-Tank Platoon/Trackers carried anti-tank weapons, and this will make you laugh…we had anti-tank weapons made in Scandinavia, but they wouldn't supply us with ammunition, so they were carrying these bloody weapons without ammunition…because Scandinavia was against the war in Vietnam.'

So, V Company and the 'Anti-Tank' Platoon were to land at a zone on Route 44. This landing zone was secured a few moments before by B Company and a troop of cavalry that travelled by road from Nui Dat. A small tactical headquarter group travelled with B Company.

At approximately 1830hrs on the 3rd of December, B Company and the APCs moved through Dat Do and swung onto the Route 44. Five minutes later they had passed Hoi My and were blocking the road to the south. B Company commenced to secure a road back to the bridge just south of the village.

It was precisely at 1840hrs that the helicopters carrying V Company and the Anti-tank platoon began to touch down. At 1845hrs a voice aircraft—which was a small Cessna plane with loud speakers that used to fly over the villages to let them know what is going on—broadcast to the villagers explaining that the village had been surrounded and would be searched the next day and everyone was to stay indoors.

The next morning the Vietnamese police and troops arrived from Baria, the capital of Phuoc Tuy Province. A screening centre was erected by 0730hrs. 'This was essentially barbed wire enclosing an area that provided shade and our medical team looking after villagers who needed medical attention at the time'. Shortly after this centre was erected, B Company began searching the village accompanied by interpreters and police. All houses were searched and after the house was searched the occupants were accompanied to the screening centre where there were checks of their ID cards and work permits. The villagers were then held in the screening centre until all buildings were searched; this was completed by 1030hrs.

In just three hours, 300 villagers were screened, and twenty-nine suspects taken back to Baria for further interrogation.

Upon completion of the search, B Company were choppered back to the Long Green to carry on Operation Forest. V Company were choppered back to the Horseshoe and the Anti-Tank platoon and tactical headquarters went back to Nui Dat.

Beneath the Southern Cross I Stand

Operation Lawley conducted from the 22nd to the 23rd of December, was another small operation conducted during Forest. Lawley was a cordon search of the village of Ngai Gia O situated on Route 2 north of the Taskforce Base of Nui Dat.

Similar to the search during Operation Canungra, Lawley was to be conducted in three phases with the main aim to search the villages of La Van and Vinh Thanh to the south of Route 2. Darryl recalls, 'On the 22nd of December B Company flew in, followed by C Company then the tactical headquarters. With D company last flown in, the whole process had only taken about thirty minutes. You used to see about twenty to thirty helicopters fly in at once to move everyone as quick as they can.'

While the fly in was going on, a road convoy was moving in carrying a screening centre, stalls and a Platoon of W Company. Darryl says, 'This was another company of Kiwis, and they must have just come in from Malaysia. It would have been not long after this that 2RAR became an ANZAC Battalion and D Company is disbanded because of all the losses they had.'

Within six hours, 1200 villagers were screened, and ninety-three persons were detained. On the 23rd of December, 2RAR was flown back to Nui Dat. [xxiii]

There were now operations within operations and the men were in and out of Nui Dat in between. The operations were all rolling into one another. The soldiers had little time to think about what they were doing on one operation as they would be entering the next. Darryl recalls during Operation Forest when they were back at Nui Dat for a short while and he heard of the disappearance of the Australian Prime Minister Harold Holt.

It was on the 17th of December that Harold Holt went missing while swimming in a beach near Portsea Victoria. Five days later the search was scaled down and his body never found.

Darryl 'Coop' Cooper

I think anyone in Australia at the time would remember what they were doing when Holt disappeared. Darryl was back in Nui Dat and listening to the news on the radio. He recalls, 'We had our forces radio—Good Morning Vietnam—they were worried that we were going to desert them because our prime minister had gone missing. Every half hour it used to come over the radio to the Australian Task Force in Vietnam to "Stay in your barracks and everything will be alright. The American army will be there to help you." They were worried we were going to surrender and go home.'

Darryl thought back to when he had met the Prime Minister in Borneo, 'I got my photo taken with Harold Holt at a market in Borneo. I can always remember he had yellow teeth. He said, "I'm not very photogenic, soldier, but I'd like to get a picture here of me and you for my home collection." I said, "Alright Sir."' Little did Darryl know at the time of standing beside the Prime Minister in Malaysia getting his picture taken, that Holt was about to set in motion some landmark policies that would shape the next fifty years in Australia. He had increased Australia's commitment to Vietnam and was the reason Darryl was in Vietnam at the time. He began dismantling the White Australia Policy and championed the historic 1967 referendum that saw Aboriginal Australians, counted in the census of which more than ninety percent of Australians voted in favour of. His disappearance was a shock to the nation and began some incredible conspiracy theories at the time.

Following Holt's disappearance, 2RAR stayed in Nui Dat for Christmas Day and for a few days after. There was no chance of them leaving Vietnam as the Americans had thought they would—they had a job to do. Although, that job was now taking its toll. In and out of operations, choppers, jungle, trenches, villages, O Groups, the men of 2RAR were starting to feel the mental and physical exhaustion of what they were enduring.

Beneath the Southern Cross I Stand

Darryl says, 'At this point in our tour...this is where more deaths started to occur because the blokes were just overworked. This was six months in, and the operations were longer, and you know...twenty-four hours a day we were going. At this stage, this is the harvest and the dry season. Although we had been fighting the Viet Cong for six months, we are about to get our arse kicked because it is not the Viet Cong we will be fighting it is the NVA and the NVA are trained soldiers... they don't run away. We expected them to and they never and that's how we had a lot of casualties. We are coming up to the '68 Tet Offensive...'

33

Operation Duntroon
10th to 21st January, 1968

Darryl says, 'Now I was to find out how hard it was to sleep at night because we are now fighting NVA. We would have to search the bodies of the dead enemy. We would find in their wallets or personal effects pictures of them in their dress uniforms with their wife and children just like us. Even the VC would dress up in their best black pyjamas with their wives and children. They used to look very proud.'

The bodies of the enemy were buried on site and the officers would mark the position where they were buried at the battlefields. The soldiers would have to assist with this task that would haunt them for years to come. During these burials and searches in Operation Duntroon, they began to find more evidence of the NVA on the battlefield.

Duntroon was a taskforce operation conducted in the North West of Phuoc Tuy Province in conjunction with Operation Akron mounted by the 1st Brigade of the 9th Infantry Division of the United States Army. The taskforce had the usual Australian support units.

Beneath the Southern Cross I Stand

The operation was conducted in the area known as the Hat Bich base which was the traditional home of the 274th Regiment of the North Vietnamese Army. Previously in this area, the US army had come across many large camps.

The role of 2RAR and 7RAR in this operation was to establish the southern blocking position and search and destroy within the area. 2RAR was also responsible for protection of the fire support base. This job was given to C Company. Additionally, 108 Field Battery was under the command of 2RAR again.

During the night before the 10th of January, A Squadron of the 3rd Cavalry Regiment prepared for the mounting of 2RAR via APCs and assault helicopters with two Chinook helicopters in support. Darryl says, 'To move a battalion of 1000 men, you can just imagine all of the equipment we needed to get us in there, plus all of our fire support units.' During this operation Whiskey Company remained at the horseshoe.

On the 10th of January, 2RAR was flown by helicopters to a concentration area which had been secured by C Company. The cavalry was at the commanded area. 2RAR was joined by 7RAR and the artillery. The next day, 2RAR flew by helicopter company and six RAAF helicopters into the landing zone Cook which was bombarded by artillery before they had landed. From the landing zone, the companies quickly moved to their objectives and by nightfall were all in position.

Battalion headquarters and a section of mortars remained in the area of the landing zone. Further north, 7RAR and fire support base reached their positions and on the 12th of January B Company moved further north by foot. Victor Company adjusted their position to form a block force more or less at right angles to the general line of the other companies. Also, while occupying these positions the companies patrolled any gaps in the blocking line. [xxiv]

Darryl 'Coop' Cooper

B Company found a tunnel complex that was an old hospital. It was about eight hundred metres long. It was the job of the pioneers and engineers to search the bunker systems. You will recall that after Borneo Darryl's mate, Cleggie, had joined the Pioneers Platoon. Darryl says, 'As part of our battalion, Cleggie was attached to our company at times. It was the pioneer's and engineer's job to go down to check the bunker systems first, not so much the infantry but if we had to, we would. So that was Cleggie's job. One day we were on patrol, and we walked past this hole and Cleggie was behind me, and I said, "Hey Cleggie, there's a hole." He said, "Don't fuckin' tell anyone."' Darryl laughs, 'I told the Corporal.' It would be a terrifying task to enter the bunker systems and tunnels of the enemy not knowing what would be waiting beneath the surface but as was their job the engineers flew in and destroyed this complex.

At 0900hrs on the same day, twenty VC walked into Victor Company ambush. A fight developed and raged for the next four hours. The American gunships were flown in the area. They also flew in a DC9 which they called 'Puff, the Magic Dragon'. Darryl explains, 'These were planes full of machineguns and the DC9 could cover a football field in one burst'. This contact ended with a large amount of VC killed. Two New Zealanders one Australian were wounded.

At 1045hrs, two VC who withdrew from the battle with Victor Company were ambushed by B Company and killed.

On the 16th of January, Victor Company had further contact which ended in further VC fatalities. The next day the brigade completed this operation and the Australian rifle companies quit their blocking positions. Victor Company joined Battalion Headquarters at the Landing Zone Cook. They swept east and were completed by the 20th with no significant contacts.

On the 19th of January, B Company had found and destroyed another tunnel system. A Company contacted more VC, but they fled before the company could fire on them. A Company captured their weapons. 'In other words,' Darryl says, 'the VC had dropped their weapons and ran.'

After 11 days, the operation concluded and 2RAR returned back to Nui Dat by helicopter.

It was at this point that the number of casualties and fatalities increased for the Australian Army. Not only were they tasked with burying the enemy, but they were also moving their mates out dead and alive on the 'dust off'. 'That's what they used to call the ambulance helicopters that come and get you. They call you a dust off.'

Darryl reflects, 'We would find out about our mates being killed and wounded at our Orders Group each day. 'O Group' we used to call it. O Group was every morning to let you know what patrols you had to do on that day.

We started to treat our boozer like a wake and would celebrate the service of the men that were killed. Sometimes our officers and sergeants would come and have a drink with us and check our wellbeing.

I would lie there at night and think back on our contacts and think why in the hell did I do that…what the Corporal would tell me to do…run over there behind a tree or get behind that log to give cover and fire with the crack of bullets going all around me. I thought, maybe it was because we wanted to protect our mates, or maybe it was the army discipline or the drills we used to do on the parade grounds day after day. Whatever it was, we were soldiers. Grunts of the mighty Bravo Company of the 2nd Battalion of the Royal Australian Regiment.'

34

My Mate, Bones
24th January to 14th February

Operation Coburg took place in the area between Bien Hoa and Long Kahn province south west of Phuoc Tuy province. Post-Christmas in this area saw an increase in enemy forces in the lead up to the Tet Offensive.

Another Battalion of the Royal Australian Regiment, 3 RAR had joined the Taskforce around Christmas time 1967. With 2RAR, 3RAR, 7RAR, the usual support units of artillery, cavalry, engineers and 161 Independent Recce Flight plus other attachments the 1st Australian Taskforce was almost at brigade strength.

This operation was unique for it marked the first time that the taskforce operated outside of the Phuoc Tuy Province. It also involved major deployments of troops over a long distance. This was accomplished in a matter of 2 days. B Company was one of the first companies in. They harboured up not far from the landing zone.[xxv]

Darryl says, 'We found elements of a VC rocket regiment moving into the area to attack the huge American complexes at Bien Hoa and Long Binh. The main aim of Coburg was to deny the VC access to the area and there were also rumours of a cease fire because

Beneath the Southern Cross I Stand

the 1968 Tet was coming up—the Vietnamese New Year Festival. B Company were very happy to hear the news and the soldiers seemed to be happy and relaxed at this time. I was thinking now that my R and R to Bangkok in a couple of weeks was something to look forward to. Just think…not being on an operation, not have to shoot anyone and not being shot at.'

Darryl recalls one day during Operation Coburg, being on a water bottle patrol. 'The platoon had a creek not far from where we were harboured. I went down to the creek to fill up the water bottles and I remember looking across the creek to the bank on the other side and never took much notice.

The next day was Australia day, 26th of January when our Company was moving out. We led the company to the water point so our platoon was up front. We stopped to have a rest when 5 Platoon came to relieve us. I was not taking much notice when I got a big boot in the arse and looked up and it was my old mate from Malaysia and Borneo—Bones Binning. He was telling me that 5 Platoon was going to lead the company now and 4 Platoon was weak as piss.'

As they were going across to the other side of the bank, the enemy were waiting on the bank on the other side. They ambushed 5 Platoon as they came through. 'All hell broke loose with 5 Platoon going to ground to fight the enemy while 6 Platoon swept through the area killing enemy as they went. Our platoon—4 Platoon were to protect the rear just in case we had a counterattack come up from the rear.

The contact went on for what felt like a long time. I knew someone was killed and others were wounded. One of the poor diggers had been shot in the lungs and the suffering…I had never ever heard anything as bad before or since. He died in the helicopter on the way to the hospital. The pain that poor bugger went through, I will never forget. I asked one bloke from 5 Platoon who else had

Darryl 'Coop' Cooper

been shot and I remember he looked up and was about to tell me then he saw who I was and said he didn't know.

After everything was completed, my platoon went up to lead the company out and as I passed through Company Headquarters, I saw Bones' extra-large boots sticking out from under this plastic sheeting and I knew it was my mate, Bones. I wanted to pay my respects, but Major Carter was behind me and told me to "Keep moving, Cooper."

Now, every time I go to Enoggera at Brisbane, I visit Bones. Kiwi Gibbons had planted trees and put a plaque at Enoggera for any soldiers killed in the Regiment. I paid for the little plaque under Bones' tree of remembrance. I always go to Bones' tree and say a little thank you for being a good mate.'

35
Dust Off

During Operation Coburg, the contact started every morning before 0900 hours and 2RAR would be in contact all day. Darryl says, 'We often felt we would never get to help the Americans around Bien Hoa and Long Binh because we got held up every day.'

On one particular day, they had the enemy trapped up in a ravine and called in the gunships. Darryl says, 'To let them know we were not mucking around. The gunships flew over our heads, and we thought they were firing at us. As Australian soldiers we never had steel helmets. So, we got our entrenching tools out to cover our heads. Everyone had their shovels out above their heads. It turned out that they were not shooting at us. It was the spent cartridges from the machineguns falling out of the gunships and coming down on top of us.'

Every night the soldiers would dig shell scrapes. Just as they had in Borneo, they would dig eighteen inches into the earth so they could lie down in it and fire out. 'We would dig the shell scrapes to protect us from the rockets which the enemy would fire at us every night. We would lie there and hear the rockets go off. You could not hear the rockets coming in. Not like artillery where you can hear the

Darryl 'Coop' Cooper

whistle when the rounds are coming in. So again, you would grind your teeth, wait a few seconds and if you felt no pain, you were pretty right. I'll never forget one night on Operation Coburg I was digging my shell scrape when my Sergeant Tom Birnie yelled out, "Don't dig it too deep, Cooper, because you have to be able to shoot and fire out of it." I yelled back, "I can still shoot out of it. I don't want to be shot in the fuckin' head!" He said, "Cooper, if you were shot in the fuckin' head you would survive because it is full of shit anyway!"

The next morning it was the 31st of January and they had been out for the last seven days. Held up and digging in for the last seven days. Darryl said, 'So much for the ceasefire we had heard rumours of.'

'I hoped this day was going to be a quiet one for it had been confirmed that my trip on the 5th of February to Bangkok was still on.'

It was about 0930hrs, and B Company was moving out with 4 Platoon (Darryl's platoon) in front. Corporal Bob Murray's Section 3 was leading, then Corporal Brian Andrew's Section 2 (Darryl's section), then Corporal Ian Atkinson's Section 1.

'All of a sudden, we were under fire again with a contact to the right side of the track. I was number two on the machinegun. The machine gunner was Ralph Hoger. I knew I had to get to him to help him with the gun. While I was running to help him, I could hear the crack of bullets around me, and leaves were being shot off around my head. Then all of a sudden something hit me and arse over tit I went. With all my equipment I was carrying, I hit this small tree with my right shoulder. My mates were jumping over me to get to the action and yelling out "Cooper's hit! Get a stretcher bearer." I heard my mate, Corporal Ian Atkinson yell out, "Coop's hit, I think he's fucked!"

The sergeant and the CSM arrived with the stretcher bearer. They were trying to bandage my head and I said my head's alright and that it was my legs giving me the pain. I remember Sergeant Birnie tending to my head before they bandaged my head. The CSM Kiwi Gibbons gave me a cigarette. Then the medic arrived.

The battle was still going on. I was still conscious and the pain and whistling in my head was unbearable. I don't know how long I waited there but it didn't seem long for I heard a helicopter above me and it was my 'dust off'. The stokes litter—wire cage with stretcher—was lowered down through the jungle. I was loaded on and winched up to the chopper. The enemy was still firing at me being winched up. Later at the reunions, my mates would joke with me saying that it was them firing at me because I was going out to have a bludge back at camp. Also, Kiwi Gibbons was always saying to me at the reunions how he gave me his last cigarette.'

That day B Company had come across a well dug-in platoon with light machineguns, automatic rifles and rocket launchers. 4 Platoon was pinned down for the next two hours. After engaging the enemy with artillery, B Company attacked position and fought from bunker to bunker. 5 Platoon was pinned down for a couple of hours by snipers. By 1700hrs the fighting had died down and by 1830hrs Victor Company had reached B Company to reinforce them.[xxvi] The battle that day had gone for nine hours straight and ended with six soldiers from B Company wounded that day, including Darryl.

Darryl says, 'Flying away on the helicopter that day, my combat experience for my 1st tour was over. Now it was up to the doctors, sisters, nurses, the medics and my brother and friends to get me through this.'

36
The Road Down Under

After he was winched up into the dust-off helicopter, the Viet Cong still shooting at him, Darryl had checked with the medical staff and found out there were no more incidents. 'Except for the American who winched me up kept eyeing off my rifle and equipment. I thought he was going to knock it off. It did not worry me, because I had more to worry about right now. My ears were still ringing, and my legs were in pain.'

They later landed at the American MASH hospital at Long Binh. This was the largest U.S. Army base in Vietnam located just outside of Saigon.

'When we landed, there were two big American negros who loaded me onto a stretcher. They then ran to this building with me on the stretcher and my equipment and rifle were taken from me. Then another two American negros ran me all the way to a place where I was X-rayed. After that, another two Americans took me to the surgery and straight to the operating table where the doctors and nurses were waiting. I was still conscious. I can always remember the sister's reaction to my stink when they cut my uniform off because I hadn't changed clothes or taken my boots off for about 10 days. I apologised for the smell. They put the gas mask on me and I was put to sleep.'

'When I woke up, I was in another ward. I reached down and to my surprise I could still feel my legs were there. I had a shaving mirror in my little locker next to my bed which I got out and I could see a big bandage around my head. I thought that I hurt my head when I fell down and hit the tree.'

Shortly after that, a doctor and nurse came to the side of Darryl's bed. The doctor cut the bandage off his head. All of a sudden, there was a siren was going off and all the staff rushed out of the hospital and into defence positions. 'The sirens were going off and I could hear in the distance, small arms fire and rocket explosions. I thought, here I go again but I had no weapons and no equipment so there was nothing I could do. I just lay there and waited for my fate.

While I was waiting, I grabbed the shaving mirror and checked my head out, because there was no bandage there now. I had a big scar right across my forehead with about a hundred stiches. I also had a small cut on my forehead. I started to think, what could have happened? I thought maybe the bullet hit the side of my head and I then moved, and the bullet ran around my head and that the cut on my forehead happened when I fell and hit the tree. I then thought I would be back with my mates in about a week's time.'

Then the sirens went off again which meant standdown. The enemy were fought off and the doctors and nurses returned. 'When they came back in—they looked ridiculous actually, they were wearing flap jackets and helmets and just didn't look right—the doctor explained what had happened. The cut on my head was when the bullet hit my head and blew a hole in my head bigger than an Aussie fifty cent coin. When this happened, it pushed into the front of my brain. I was told that the righthand side of your brain controls the left-hand side of your body and vice versa. So, when it hit the nerves at the front of my brain it effected my legs. That explained why my legs hurt a lot. I didn't realise it, but I didn't have much pain in my legs then. The scar on the top of my head is where they had cut inside my hairline to bring the top of my face down to remove the bullet and the broken bone. I lay back in shock and said to the doctors, "In other words I won't be going back to my mates next week?" Little did I know that I would be in hospital for the next nine months before I was discharged.'

Darryl was laying in hospital and was just dozing off when a hand shook him. He looked up, and it was his brother, Errol, who at that time was in the navy. Errol was on the *HMAS Sydney* at the time Darryl was wounded. 'He had a couple of tins of beer down the front of his shirt and wanted to give me one, but I didn't feel like it at the time. He was in an army uniform which was two sizes too big for him. The Australian Navy was not allowed on Vietnam soil.'

Errol says of the day he arrived at Long Binh, 'There were two lines of tents. The first line is where they don't expect you to recover and that's where Darryl was. Darryl woke up and recognised me.' Darryl doesn't remember this day. 'The next day when I went to see him, he was in the recovery ward. Darryl was shot just outside of Long Binh, so it only took thirty minutes to get to this hospital. He was very lucky because he had the best neurosurgeon at this American hospital.'

Errol explained to Darryl that their parents had received a telegram that he was wounded. That the local policeman, the local padre and an army major delivered the telegram to his family home in Rockhampton. They had knocked on the front door and when Darryl's Mum opened the door she just screamed. 'The telegram let them know that I had received a gunshot wound at 0930hrs the morning of the 31st of January 1968. Apparently, Dad got onto the president of the Rockhampton RSL – the Rockhampton RSL have always looked after me - who then got onto the navy in Melbourne and got Errol off the *Sydney* to be beside me. There was a small write up in the Rockhampton paper at the time that they titled 'Brothers in Arms'.

'I was also told Mum used to go to bed with my photo every night—the photo of me with my army slouch hat on.' It must have been hard on Darryl's mum with all three boys away at war. Hard on every parent and family member who received news of their loved ones injured or killed on duty. Because every family member endures the shock and the grief of the news. Darryl's sister, Val, says of the time, 'I was living in New Zealand when I got the news, I had just had my son, Garth. When I heard what had happened, I was in shock, and I instantly lost my milk.'

Then, for every family member back home hearing of their wounded son, brother, father or nephew, there is the wait. Waiting for news from thousands of miles away. Waiting for news of recovery and if their boy is going to make it back to them.

It was also hard on the close friends of those in Vietnam. They would also bear the burden of fear, grief and loss for their friends who were wounded or killed. Back in Canungra, Australia, on the day Darryl was shot, Darryl's mate Andy was taken out of a line up by 4RAR CSM, Jock Richardson, and was told, "Cooper has been shot and is in a pretty bad way." Andy was kept up to date every day with how Darryl was doing.

Darryl had found out years later in the welcome home march in Sydney in 1987 that there was a Lieutenant that was shot in the shoulder the day Bones Binning was killed. He was also at Long Binh hospital and used to visit Darryl to see how he was, and he would let B Company know how Darryl was coming along. Darryl says, 'He reckons that I seemed to be away in the clouds at the time he came to see me. I could not remember him.'

While there would have been a lot Darryl didn't remember of his hospital visit due to the trauma of his head injury, there were a number of things he recalls of his stay over the couple of weeks he was admitted at the American Long Binh hospital.

He says, 'I remember, there was this little Puerto Rican who had one stripe and I called him a corporal. He quickly turned around and he said, "Hey Aussie, I am only a Private 1st Class". I said to him, "In our army a soldier with one stripe is a lance corporal and we call them corporals, so I am going to call you corporal."

Well, this little bloke couldn't do enough for me. He used to make sure that my bed space and bed was immaculate and that I had plenty of water and ice.

I remember one day I watched this American major going to each bed shaking their hands and putting something on their PJs. Then he came to me to give me something. He looked up at my bed tag which stated Australian Regular Army. He excused himself and went to the next bed. I found out he was giving out Purple Heart Medals.

Another night, I had just got to sleep when this nurse started mucking around with these drips hanging out of me and I lost my temper and swore at her. The next morning the same nurse was still on duty, and she went to my brother and told him that I had a foul mouth. Errol turned around and said, "I taught him everything he fuckin' knows." She left with her nose in the air mumbling, "Damn Australians."

Darryl did not feel comfortable in the Long Binh hospital because he says, 'The Americans just laid in their beds staring into space.' An Australian padre used to visit Darryl and one day, Darryl turned to him and said, "Have a look at these poor bloody wounded Americans. They have no will to live. Could I be transported to the Australian hospital at Vung Tau." The padre looked around and said to him, "I understand what you mean."

Within a few days Darryl was transferred to the Australian hospital at Vung Tau. 'And this starts another bad chapter of my life.'

Part 5

The Long Road Home

Sitting by a fire in the middle of the bush you are mesmerised. Eyes locked on the dancing flames; you hear only the crackling of the fire. The warmth radiating from the flames gently touches your cheeks and seems to seep into your body, warming and relaxing every muscle as it does. When you break your locked gaze to look up to the sky you see millions of stars illuminated by the darkness of the outback. Your gaze fixes on the Southern Cross. You feel the comfort in these moments of familiarity.

Darryl 'Coop' Cooper

37
The Next Bad Chapter of My Life

'You think life is going to get better. It can't get any worse. But then it does.'

In the back of a medivac chopper again, Darryl was being transferred from Long Binh US Army base to 8th Field Ambulance Hospital, Vung Tau. 'It was good to be back again with Australian medics who made me feel more at home. I was put into ICU in Vungas straight away and felt more relaxed and comfortable. The hospital was overloaded. They had tents up to accommodate all the wounded. My brother came back with us.'

Now that he was back at 8th Field Ambulance Hospital, Darryl had a lot of visitors whom he hardly remembers. 'I was surprised to find out a few of my mates from B Company were also in the hospital. I recognised some of my mates who had been wounded. Corporal Bob Murray was there, he had malaria and some other blokes from the company. Also, I found out years later that I had a lot of visitors. My cousin, Bob, came to visit me from 7RAR, and other mates that I had served with in my army career. I don't remember how many days I was in 8th Field Ambulance, but we had to wait for a RAAF Hercules hospital plane out of Vietnam.'

Beneath the Southern Cross I Stand

Then the day came when they left Vietnam. Around twenty of the injured men, including Darryl, were loaded onto medivac choppers this time headed for the RAAF base at Butterworth in Malaysia. 'When we arrived, I was placed in a ward near the beach. I enjoyed my stay there and started to feel a whole lot better. I don't remember how long I was there for. Errol was still with me.'

The next flight was homeward bound. 'I was put onto another hospital Herc, and this time we were flying back to Australia. The doctors, sisters and nurses on these planes treated us very well. We landed in Australia with a roar and a clap of our hands with appreciation and relief as we landed at Richmond Air Base.'

After landing Darryl was approached by a RAAF airman who later explained that his name was Polly Perkins and his brother lived next door to Darryl's parents in Rockhampton. Polly was able to let his parents know that he had landed back in Australia and was alright.

The men were then loaded into several army ambulances. With lights flashing and sirens blaring the military police escorts transported them to 2 Camp Hospital at Ingleburn. Ingleburn, where Darryl first completed his Infantry Corps Training. Darryl laughs, 'What goes around, comes around.'

'At Ingleburn, there were volunteers waiting beside our beds to help us fill out our forms so we could receive a pension as soon as possible. My brother was then transferred back to his naval unit. I stayed in the army hospital in Ingleburn until they could fly me back to Brisbane on a commercial TAA flight. Finally, after a week they sent me home. I boarded the TAA flight with everyone staring at me. I didn't mind, I was going home to Queensland. I wondered what awaited me there.'

Darryl's section commander, Brian Andrews, was engaged to Claudette, a girl who lived in Darryl's Street in Rockhampton. Brian had asked Claudette to let Darryl's parents know of his progress. 'When we had landed at the Brisbane airport, Claudette and her

Darryl 'Coop' Cooper

friend, Anne, were waiting for me. I was then taken out to 1 Camp Hospital at Yeronga on the Brisbane River where I started my months of really hard rehabilitation.' Claudette and Anne visited Darryl every day and sent word back to his parents to let them know how he was progressing.

Heavily drugged and with a serious head wound, this period of hospital transfers and treatment remains a blur for Darryl. He was unsure of how long he spent at the Vung Tau and Malaysian hospitals. He had not yet had any more operations since the bullet was removed at Long Binh. Finally, back in Queensland, he says 'Now the hard recovery started. This is where the pain started all over again.'

38
My Little Pork Pie

Back in Australia Darryl says, 'Everything seemed to be different…and safe. The weather was starting to feel a bit fresh.'

Yeronga Military Hospital, Brisbane was an old army hospital used in the Second World War. 'It was nice and clean, tidy and comfortable.'

He was only in ICU for a few days then taken out to the ward where there were more wounded soldiers from Vietnam. 'A lot of them had been mine casualties with limbs missing but they were also well drugged up.'

Back in the ward started a gruelling process of tests and examinations working towards his major head operation. Darryl had doctors examine him during their rounds every morning. With a nurse escort, he was sent to specialists around Brisbane to have various tests on his brain.

During the hospital stay, the Vietnam wounded were still able to get their two can beer ration every night. 'We had to go outside so we didn't drink in front of the other patients.' During his recovery, Darryl's old mate, Andy, visited him in hospital. It was the 27th of February 1968—the night that Lionel Rose fought Harada in Tokyo

Darryl 'Coop' Cooper

and won the world title. A turning point in Australia's history as Rose was the first Indigenous person to be named Australian of the Year and this was less than twelve months since the 1967 referendum on Indigenous rights.

Darryl laughs, 'Andy had brought a bottle of rum with him hidden down his shirt. Anyway, we listened to the fight on the wireless and we got pissed. Andy had to be escorted out of the hospital by the military police and I got a lecture off the matron the next day.'

Between his medical appointments, the doctors would also send Darryl home for a few days leave.

The first time he went home to Rockhampton was on a week's leave. He says, 'I had not contacted my parents during this time because I felt ashamed about being wounded.' He remembers the taxi pulling up in front of the house. The lady over the road was visiting. 'As soon as she saw me, she left. All I had in my possession was the uniform I had on, and I had a Red Cross bag which had all of my shaving gear in it. My mum opened the door, and I came in and she just started crying. She could not see the wound because it was bandaged. My sister, Dianne, came home and then later, my father. That night nothing came up about the war. Only about how I was now feeling.

I would meet my dad after work at the pub and we would never talk about the war, but all his mates would say how well we were doing over there. My old mates where I worked at Southern Cross could only say "We told you to keep your fuckin' head down!" Some of them were Second World War veterans. I caught up with some old school buddies also. The week at home was very relaxing.'

Darryl returned to 1 Camp Hospital, Yeronga and to more specialist visits around Brisbane. 'I was beginning to feel like a show pony.' Finally, the day came when there was a plan for his operation. The neurosurgeon in Brisbane told Darryl he would have to send to

Germany for a bone which was especially bred in a calf for the type of operation Darryl needed. He told Darryl it would take a few weeks to arrive and asked what he would like to do—wait in hospital or go on home on leave. Darryl says, 'Guess what I chose?'

'I never wore the bandage at this time, and you could see the wound. During the day if I had high blood pressure you would not know there was a hole there but low blood pressure the skin would go back into my head, and you would see the hole. My father asked me to buy a hat to cover the hole and so I bought a little pork pie hat that I then wore everywhere I went. I will never forget my little pork pie hat.'

During this longer leave break, Darryl's mum suggested he go to Sydney to see how his ex-girlfriend Carol and the baby were going. Scott had been born two years prior when he was in Borneo. He knew that he had been born because Carol had written to Darryl's mother.

Darryl flew to Sydney and arrived at Seven Hills. He knocked on the door of Carol's house. He recalls, 'A woman came out who must have been her mother. I said, "Is Carol home?" She said, "No, she's at work. Who wants to know?" I said, "Darryl Cooper." She said she'll be back at such and such a time. So, I left. When I came back, and Carol opened the door and here's this little baby sitting in the lounge room behind her playing. I asked if she needed any help, any financial assistance. She said, "No, I'm getting married Saturday."'

'I flew back to Rockhampton hoping the little boy would be alright. My mum was not happy because she would have loved to have seen him. We both thought leaving them alone would be the best for both of them.'

39
Operation Save My Life

'It was time for me to get back to the hospital and to have this operation which I was praying would happen to find out how much it had affected me.'

Darryl returned to more appointments with his specialist who loved to joke around with him. They got along well.

'I remember my mother had the dates wrong and she rang the hospital the day before the operation to find out how everything went. My poor mum now had to go through another day of waiting.'

The day of Darryl's operation had finally come. He remembers lying on the operating table. 10, 9, 8, 7…

When it was over and he came to, all he remembers of the time is craving orange juice which the nurse brought to him. It didn't stay down long and there was a panic across the ward as he was being sick. Here began the next phase of his recovery.

It was not long after the operation that the minister for the army, Mr Lynch, came to visit the hospital. 'I can always remember this young lieutenant in the bed opposite who got up early in the morning to make sure his bed space was perfect for the visit.' Darryl laughs, 'When the minister came to our section, he asked the doctor

"What is wrong with the lieutenant?" and the doctor replied, "He is in here to have an operation to remove his appendix." The minister said, "We won't waste time here then" and he walked over to me and asked how I was going and if I was getting excellent treatment. I replied that I was.'

Darryl was then interviewed by reporters and articles were published in the *Brisbane Courier Mail* and later in the *Australian Post* magazine, 11th of July 1968 along with a photo of Darryl and the minister for the army. 'The next time I visited this brilliant neurosurgeon he got up me jokingly because I didn't mention his name in the interview. Dr Tokely, I think his name was. He was a great bloke.'

It was now coming into May and Darryl knew that his battalion would be home soon. 'Safe, and ready for a few weeks' leave. Thinking over my time in hospital over the months I was looking forward to being discharged from the hospital and back to my unit.'

It was getting close to 2RAR return to Australia and the commanding officer of the hospital had told Darryl that they wanted him on the saluting dais when the battalion marched through Brisbane. 'They told me that I had to go in a wheelchair. Also, they had a couple of nurses escort me.'

Then the day had come, 13th of June 1968. 2RAR disembarked the *HMAS Sydney* and were trucked into Brisbane city. Darryl says, 'I was sitting on the dais in my wheelchair when I heard the band strike up playing 2, 3s. The RSM and the CSMs were shouting the command to quick march. I had tears in my eyes as the battalion started marching down Queen St, Brisbane. A Company was first, then B Company and when B Company gave an "eyes left" they gave me a wink and a big smile. I was happy they were now safe and there was no more horror for them. But some of their troubles had just started.' For this is where the nightmares would begin. 'The nurse would not let me stand to attention because they were still worried about me. Then the band started to play *Ringo* which was our regimental march, and our colours were marching past.'

When Darryl went back to the hospital that day, the nurses let him have a couple of beers. He stayed in that hospital for a while as his head was healing. He was recovering well, and the doctors had said that as soon as the stitches were out, he could go on leave again. 'I remember the nurse there... the one who took my stiches out.' He laughs, 'She said to me she did not know how she would go because she had a big night on the rum and coke the night before. But she got the job done. The stiches were out, and I went on leave.'

It wasn't long after the operation that Darryl marched out of 1 Camp Hospital. It had been nine months since he had first been admitted to hospital. It was now September 1968. With all his documents he marched straight back into 2RAR who were based at Enoggera.

When asked why Darryl went straight back—after being shot in the head and so close to death, and then enduring a long and gruelling nine months of pain, doctors' appointments, specialists, tests, more pain and a major operation unsure if there would be ongoing brain damage, he simply replies, 'It was my job, I was a soldier.'

Beneath the Southern Cross I Stand

Articles from Rockhampton Courier Mail

Australia Post, 11 July, 1968

Darryl 'Coop' Cooper

Darryl on the saluting dais preparing for 2RAR return with General Sir Thomas Daly, 13th June 1968

Darryl on the saluting dais watching as 2RAR marched through Brisbane

40
Farewell Again…

'I marched up to the orderly room at 2RAR and handed my documents over. I was back in 2RAR. 2RAR at this stage had only a few men—skeleton staff because the Nashos had been discharged and some of the regulars had enough and so got their discharges too. They attached me to C Company because they were going to New Zealand the officers thought it would be a good break for me to go.'

When New Zealand had committed to the Vietnam war during Darryl's 1st tour, V Company from the 1st Battalion Royal New Zealand Infantry Regiment (RNZIR) was attached to 2RAR as a fifth rifle company. V Company was relieved by W Company in December 1967. New Zealand also had a major who came in as 2IC. Darryl says, 'We become the first ANZAC Company since the First World War. Of all the battalions there were only three ANZAC Battalions, 2RAR, 4RAR, 6RAR.'

C Company arrived in Auckland, New Zealand in September 1968 for training with the New Zealand army. After a few days in Auckland, Darryl decided to visit his sister, Val, who was living in One Tree Hill, Auckland. 'I told her that I just arrived, and she said "Liar! We saw you on TV arriving at the Auckland airport."'

Darryl 'Coop' Cooper

'We had a good time in Auckland for a few days and then we were bussed down to the training area in Waioru. It was very cold over there and we were not much help because we froze. We did an exercise there, but it had to be called off because it was too cold for us. Don't forget the battalion had just spent twelve months in the heat of Vietnam.'

'We had taken the best rugby union players over there, but the Kiwis still gave us a hiding. The Kiwis put on a big hangi for us. We all had a great time even though they flogged us in the footy. We found that the New Zealand army was outstanding at organising anything, social and military. Better than our army. They were extraordinary! I just couldn't believe it: the shooting range, the exercises, the equipment they gave you, the hangis and the footy matches. And it's not just the army. It is the whole community that comes together!'

During Darryl's time in New Zealand the OC of C Company sent for him. 'I fronted up and he said, "Private Cooper, do you know you have been AWOL for the last couple of weeks." I said, "No, sir, I've been here." He said, "When you left the hospital you were supposed to take your documents to Duntroon in Canberra to become a storeman." What I actually did was I marched myself back into 2RAR. My mate, Lofty Horn, was the orderly room corporal and he just said, "Coop, welcome back!" and he put my paperwork through. I never showed at Duntroon, so I was classified as AWOL down there. The OC sorted it out. The Army really looked after me now.'

The men of 2RAR returned back to Brisbane and started to settle in again with training. 2RAR was building up again with both regular and national service soldiers back in the battalion. Darryl was back in B Company. 'Because of my injuries I had to be in the transport platoon, I was not able to be a rifleman.'

They were soon told that the battalion was moving to Townsville and would train to do a second tour in Vietnam from

Beneath the Southern Cross I Stand

1970 to 1971. They reported to headquarters at Lavarack Barracks, Townsville after Christmas leave in 1968. '1969 was going to be full-on because we had a new Colonel Church who was a bit different from Chicka Charlesworth.'

The coming months involved training in the mountains around Townsville and at the exercise area at Shoalwater Bay in Rockhampton. Darryl was sent to Brisbane to do a T109 truck course. This course involved training on how keep the trucks going without breaking down. Darryl recalls, 'But in those days it was only fuel and sparks. We would have to know how an engine works plus the gearbox and all the other components that kept the truck on the road.' They were taught how to recover a vehicle if it was bogged and how to use all the truck wenches. They learned how to load, and tie knots. They were trained in convoy driving and as part of this training drove around Queensland in convoy. Darryl remembers that he was at this course in Brisbane when Neal Armstrong landed on the moon on 20th July 1969.

Darryl says, 'I was nominated as the cook, so I had to cook for about fifteen blokes. We had a ten-man ration pack, and I would use two of them. I would stew everything up. We would go to the nearest town and buy a few loaves of bread and butter. The men used to love my stew. They used to call me "Cooky". What they didn't know was that I would throw everything in from the ration packs, fruit salad tins, the lot and I would curry everything up. The only thing that gave me away was the passion fruit seeds out of the fruit tins.'

When the time came to return to Townsville after the training, Darryl's old Battalion 4RAR were also moving to Townsville. He was sent to 4RAR because they were short of drivers. He says, 'So I had to be back and drive for my old battalion. It was a great job. I really enjoyed it. The transport officer was my platoon commander in Malaysia, Lieutenant Sheedy. When I got to Lavarack my old corporal, Killer Kinane, was now a staff sergeant. All my old mates

Darryl 'Coop' Cooper

from Malaysia came to greet me. Again, what goes around, comes around.'

Now it was 1970. The battalion was ready to go overseas. Darryl says, 'Mum wasn't happy.' He laughs, 'She always told me that if I was ever going to go back that she would ring my Colonel up. So, I didn't tell her I was going to Vietnam until the week before we left. Then I told her that I was only going over driving trucks and I wouldn't be in the frontline anymore…that I wasn't going to go outside the wire. She still wasn't too happy.'

The 2nd Battalion of the Royal Australian Regiment was ready to go to Vietnam again. There was a farewell parade held for the soldiers going to Vietnam and a farewell march through Townsville.

41
Back to the Pearly Gates

As more time went on, the Australian public support of the Vietnam war that had been experienced ten years previously when troops were first deployed, was now steadily declining. The number of lives lost seemed to now outweigh the strategic assertion of the domino theory. Some would argue that the media coverage fed to the television sets in Australian homes for the first time saw the steady decline in the support for the war in Vietnam. Graphic images of the fighting in the 1968 Tet offensive, the attacks on the American embassy in Saigon, the battle of Khe Sanh, the execution of a Viet Cong officer, the Kent State massacre were all broadcast to the living rooms of our homes giving us a reality of war in real time never seen before in history.[xxvii]

By 1969, when Darryl was preparing for his second tour in Vietnam, the anti-war protests across the US and Australia had gained fierce momentum. During 1970-71, when he was on his second tour in Vietnam, the moratorium marches would be held across the country. Some would argue that this increase in public dissent led to the turning point in the Vietnam War and the American and Australian withdrawal of troops in Vietnam.

Darryl 'Coop' Cooper

Darryl says, 'The second tour was different to the first because the Allies were trying to give more responsibility to the South Vietnamese so that the Allies could withdraw from South Vietnam.' Coined "Vietnamisation" the focus was now on training the South Vietnamese and the withdrawal of our troops. Introduced by Nixon in 1968, by the time Darryl was on his second tour in 1970, many changes had taken place. Most noticeably for Darryl, operations were different. On the first tour they would operate in battalion strength in company groups. Now they were down to working in company strength and platoon groups. He says, 'It was more "search and destroy" and no village searches.'

It was May 1970 and 2RAR were on their way again to South Vietnam. They were not boarding the Vung Tau Ferry but were flown over by QANTAS. Darryl says, 'How could I get in trouble this time?' He was remembering back to his first tour when he got seven days CB and ran the deck of the *HMAS Sydney*.

Before they left Australia, they were ordered to buy and carry a civilian shirt. Darryl says, 'The plane was flying to Vietnam from Townsville via Darwin and Singapore. We drank the plane dry by the time we got to Darwin where we stopped and stayed there long enough for the plane to be refuelled and then headed for Singapore. After landing in Singapore, we found out what the shirts were for. We had to take our military shirts off and put on the civilian shirts. It must have looked quite a spectacular scene to see over a hundred blokes with everyone wearing the same shoes and military pants with civilian shirts disembarking off an Australian plane in the middle of the Vietnam War.'

Boarding the QANTAS flight again, 2RAR left Singapore and headed for Saigon, South Vietnam. 'On the way I was thinking who would be stupid enough to go over here again. I looked around, I had been attached to B Company and there were a couple of my mates who had no brains also; Dave Mansfield and Chris Cannan who were with me in the first tour. I also believe that the CSM, Taffy Burke, was also on the first tour but he was with C Company.'

As the plane flew over South Vietnam Darryl looked out to see the familiar sight of bomb craters everywhere and the horrors of the first tour started coming back to him. 'The contacts, my mates dying and being wounded.' They landed at Tan Son Nhat Airport, Saigon. The airport was one of the busiest airports in the world at the time. It had traffic lights on the runways and military planes were taking off every couple of minutes. He says, 'The familiar smell of Vietnam came back to me. It was not long before we were flying into Nui Dat. Coming into Luscombe Field, I could make out the line of tents of the 1st Australian Task Force and the wire around Nui Dat. Also, the jungle beyond.'

They disembarked at Luscombe Field and then boarded trucks to the lines. As they were getting off the trucks, 6RAR was getting on. As was the tradition of the departing battalion, 'They were rubbing it in saying that we had 365 days and a wakey to go.'

Darryl was trucked to admin lines where the transport compound and living quarters was. You will remember Admin was made up of medics, truck drivers, cooks and Q-Store. Different to the support company who were the front line, mortars, Assault Pioneers, Engineers etc. Darryl says, 'In admin company, the only people who came from another corp, were the cooks and the medics. They were trained in their own corp. Q-Store and Transport Platoon were all ex-infantry blokes and generally these jobs were given to blokes who had done a good job and needed a rest.'

Darryl was allotted his tent and was soon out in the transport compound to be allotted his vehicle. He was given a Mark 5 international water truck. 'There were two water trucks and my mate, Billy Hitchcliffe, was to drive the other. We were allotted companies that we had to supply water to. Mainly the cookhouses, the showers and the toilet facilities. We settled in and that night I laid there

Darryl 'Coop' Cooper

thinking. I wondered if I would ever see the Southern Cross again. I also wondered what people back home thought of me and the only conclusion I could come up with was that I was a bloody idiot.'

The next day Darryl was in his water truck going down to the water point for the first time. He had been instructed what to do by his transport corporals. He says, 'I also had a digger with me to help with the hoses. I was sort of my own boss. Once the company had their supply of water, I could knock off and go to my tent.'

Transport platoon also had to carry out guard duties around Admin Company. They had to "stand to" at morning and night. They would do clearing patrols if the companies were out and were called on to do TAOR patrols. TAOR—Tactical Area of Responsibility—as previously explained was the patrol of an area outside the wire to prevent the enemy setting up mortar or arterial bases. Darryl says, 'So, when Admin Company went on TAORs, these blokes being ex-infantry were trained; they knew what to do. The cooks and medics were also trained out on exercises before they arrived in Vietnam. If we ever got run over, they also needed to know how to protect themselves. We still had to carry rifles and a lot of admin blokes used to carry pistols.'

B Company was on Darryl's route and driving around he says, 'I could not find much different to what it was on the first tour. The boozer still looked the same. But now they had an empty swimming pool that 6RAR had left behind. It was an above ground pool that someone in Australia donated to them. In my spare time, I would take a load of water and dump it in the pool. It took me a couple of months to fill it up.'

'It was a good job being a water truck driver, and if me and my offsider got stuck into it, we could go down to watch a concert at Luscombe Field when our work was done.'

The weeks dragged along, and Darryl started to feel guilty driving a water truck while his mates were out fighting the enemy in the jungle. 'Some nights I would go down to the operation tent and listened to the boys out in the jungle on the radio sending back sit reps (Situation Report). They would say what happened that day, how much ammo they had left all that sort of stuff. Some reminded me of my first tour.'

At this point, Darryl says, 'Little did I know that everything was about to change for me.'

42
There Were Days Like These

The Transport Compound was situated in a more central area of Nui Dat. The officers and Senior NCOs would have to pass the Transport Compound to get to Battalion Headquarters (O Groups). At times, Darryl would be in the compound when they were passing. He would often chat with them because he knew them from the first tour and had trained with them during the last couple of years.

'One of the Senior NCO's was my old Platoon Sergeant, Tom Birnie. I would often ask him how B Company was going and particularly 4 Platoon. He would tell me how they were settling in okay but told me that this tour was different from the first. He said that the contacts were the same, but the patrolling was different. He said that the men were doing 'okay'. 'Okay' I thought to myself. They should have been doing a lot better than that at this stage. We were a couple of months in now.'

Passing Transport Compound on one particular day, Tom asked Darryl if he would like to go back to 4 Platoon. He gave Darryl a couple of days to think about it. Darryl says, 'I accepted. Tom said to give him a few days to talk to the OC, Major Hoffman. He would

Beneath the Southern Cross I Stand

later talk to the CO, Lieutenant Colonel Church. Everyone agreed that I was to go back to 4 Platoon B Company.'

Sergeant Birnie and Corporal Mansfield introduced Darryl to his new platoon mates and his new platoon commander, Lieutenant McNamara. He says, 'Then I ended up in the same bed and the same tent as the first tour.'

It wasn't long after that when Darryl was out on patrol one day that a message came back to him, "Tell Sunray of 2 1 Alfa that he is now a corporal." Darryl says of this time, 'They made me up while I was out there. They marched me to take command of 1 Section. I felt a bit guilty at first because they had their lance corporal, but the corporals were heading back to Australia, and they thought with my experience that I would be a great benefit to the section who were already good, efficient and exceptional blokes.'

Then it was the usual that afternoon; malaria parade, sleeves down and to the boozer to meet the other men of B Company. 'I got to know my new blokes pretty well as well as the other blokes in the Platoon. There was one bloke there who was one of my mates from Ingleburn and from the first tour, Chris Cannan. We had a few cans that night.'

The next day the men were up early for malaria parade and to work out the jobs for each of Darryl's men in the section. 'Most of them wanted to have their old jobs back. We seemed to be getting along well together. My platoon commander and my platoon sergeant got me aside and explained what was expected of me. Now I had to brush up on my map reading and contact drills to make them perfect and get the men to brush up on their weapons skills which they were already good at anyway.'

It was time for Darryl's first operation as section commander. This was a mission to find and destroy the enemy and Darryl says, 'to bring the men back alive.' They were now working at platoon-size patrols and sometimes at company strength. Even at platoon

Darryl 'Coop' Cooper

size, they were not far away from the other platoons just in case the enemy was overwhelming them, and they needed help.

Some of the work was only section-size patrol. They would be given a grid reference to search. This would be a grid square on a map of 1000 meters by 1000 metres and the search of the grid would be conducted in a 'Z'. They would go straight across the grid and then cross it diagonally and back across again. The grid was thoroughly searched. 'We would find old enemy camps, some VC who were not abiding by the curfew that we would capture and send back to the authorities. We did come across a working hospital once. We were kept very busy again. There were also big contacts up in the Courtenay Rubber Plantation.'

There was one day of the second tour that haunts Darryl to this day. They had been in contact with the enemy for around three or four days and had just taken out a Vietcong position. They were getting short on ammunition and the platoon commander told Darryl to take his section across the creek. He was told to go down 1000 yards to look for where they could get helicopters in to resupply them with ammunition.

Darryl said, "Righto."

Tom Birnie asked, "Coop can I come with you?" and Darryl replied, "Yeah, mate, just tag along". So, they went across the creek and down 1000 yards on the other side. They then radioed back to tell the platoon commander that they were coming across the creek again.

When they got across the other side there were a couple of big tracks there and Tom said, "We'll have to send a patrol down this afternoon to see where these tracks lead to, there might be another Vietcong position here."

Darryl said, "We better take a bearing on it," and as he leaned over to take a bearing, the next thing he heard was a machinegun opening up. One of the rounds grazed his arm but two of the rounds got Tom straight in the chest. Tom went down and all he could say was, "The bastards have shot me in the back." He was trying to get up and Darryl quickly got on top of him so he couldn't get up.

Darryl then went through sixty rounds, and he used to carry full magazines in his shirt pocket. To this day he doesn't remember changing the magazines but there were three empty magazines after the contact and the machine gunner also went through three hundred.

They chopped Tom out to hospital and he died that night.

Darryl was so affected by that day that he was flown out at the same time to Saigon to be Guard Commander of Hotel Canberra in Saigon for a break. He returned to duty at Nui Dat a few days later.

He says, 'Like most bad days our platoon carried on. Tom was a good sergeant and a good friend. He had saved my life in the first tour when I was shot, and he pulled the bone from my head before they bandaged me up. Tom's death still plays on my mind to this day.'

Darryl says of the second tour, 'Most of the routine activities back at Nui Dat with the malaria parade, sleeves down, run out of beer at the boozer and day-to-day activities were similar to the first tour. Myself, Dave Mansfield, Chris Cannan and Jock Cassidy reckon the operations in both tours were completely different but the horrors happening were the same.'

There were days like the first tour where they would lie in their trenches in the grips of both fear and adrenaline listening to the explosion of artillery rounds and artillery shells whistling by. Worse still was when they couldn't hear the rockets until they heard them explode in the trees nearby. Like the first tour, they would then grind their teeth and wait to see if any of the shrapnel would hit them. After five to ten seconds, if they felt no pain, they would know they were okay.

Darryl 'Coop' Cooper

There were days like the first tour out on long operations where they would be held up for days on end, exhaustion taking over until they could finally head back to Nui Dat.

There were days like the first tour that their mates would be wounded or killed and ended in night upon night of holding wakes in the boozer.

There were days where they just counted down the days until they were home again.

Days like these would replace their dreams with nightmares.

43
Homeward Bound

After another long twelve months, finally, it was only a wakey to go and 2RAR were to board the Vung Tau Ferry—*HMAS Sydney* the next day. They were relieved by 4RAR in May 1971.

There was a lot of excitement around Nui Dat as the battalion was packing up to leave Vietnam.

'It had been a difficult year, but we had made it. When we were boarding the *Sydney*, everyone had a grin on their faces and looked to the future.'

They sailed through Indonesia and then through the Torres Strait. A speed boat came out of the area of Cape York and waved at them, and everyone waved back. They were soon anchored off Magnetic Island could see Townsville. The customs and Australian officials had boarded the boat at Cairns, and they were cleared to disembark. They had to land on the beaches at Townsville on the Second World War landing crafts because the harbour was not big enough for the *HMAS Sydney*. 'When we landed everyone was smiling and had a tear in their eye and looked at each other as if to say, 'We made it, we are home.' Darryl had an aunty who lived in Townsville who came down to welcome him home.

Darryl 'Coop' Cooper

2RAR then marched through Townsville as everyone was cheering and yelling "Well done, lads!" After the march they loaded on trucks again and out to Lavarack Barracks, handed their weapons in, got paid and were issued leave passes.

Darryl went to see Tom Burnie's wife, Joan, who was still living in Townsville and told her what had happened the day that her husband was killed. 'She seemed to be relieved after I told her the truth about what happened that day.'

Darryl headed home to Rockhampton.

44
The End of a Chapter

After a few weeks' leave Darryl returned to 4 Platoon B Company 2RAR at Lavarack Barracks. They had heard that the Australian Army was starting to withdraw from Vietnam and 4RAR was to be the last Battalion there.

'My old mates, Dave Mansfield and Alan 'Pop' Norman, were in the same platoon and we were told that we would be the next battalion to go to Singapore so it looked like I would be on my way again overseas.' At the time, and similar to, when Darryl returned from the first tour, there were only a few troops left because most of the National Servicemen and some of the Regulars had taken their discharge.

The year was 1972 and the Federal elections were coming up. The Australian Labour Party swept into power. With Gough Whitlam as Prime Minister, National Service was immediately suspended. Darryl says, 'We had to warn the Nashos not to leave straight away because they had to be demobbed by the army. In other words, properly discharged. They were given offers to be discharged or to join the Regular Army which a lot of them did.' In July 1973, the Whitlam Government passed the National Service Termination Act.

Darryl 'Coop' Cooper

The Regiment was reduced from nine battalions to six battalions. They were 1RAR, 2/4RAR, 3 RAR, 5/7RAR, 6 RAR and 8/9RAR. Singapore was cancelled. 1RAR who was in Singapore at the time came back to Lavarack Barracks.

Darryl says, 'We were really a peacetime army now and spent time training CMF (Citizen Military Forces) and Skilled Cadets at Townsville, Charters Towers and Rockhampton.

It was in January 1973 that representatives from the US, North and South Vietnam and the Vietcong signed a peace agreement in Paris. This meant a ceasefire in Vietnam, the release of all prisoners of war and ended the US involvement in Vietnam…and consequently that of Australia.

The peace was short lived. Within three weeks of US ground troop withdrawal, North Vietnam had violated the agreement and began their attacks. A paved highway was built to move tanks, trucks and a pipeline for fuel to South Vietnam.

The next two years saw the decline in the South Vietnamese Army (ARVN) as pay cuts led to soldiers leaving the ARVN and in December 1974 Le Duan organised a test attack on South Vietnam to see if the US would return. The US did nothing. North Vietnam overtook the cities and in March 1975 North Vietnam entered South Vietnam's second largest city—Da Nang. An estimated 75,000 civilians and 16,000 soldiers fled South Vietnam. Due to the large numbers of refugees and the logistical nightmare, there is tragic footage of those trying to escape by boat.

On the 27th of April, North Vietnam conducted its main assault and rockets landed on Saigon. The US President Gerald Ford gave the order for the final evacuation. On the 29th of April, Tun San Airport was bombed. A message was broadcast from Saigon and the coded message was announced on the radio, 'The temperature in Saigon is 105 degrees and rising' then the song, *White Christmas,* played. This signalled the final withdrawal from Vietnam on the 30th

Beneath the Southern Cross I Stand

of April, when the last American was lifted off the roof of the embassy. North Vietnamese tanks smashed through the gates of the presidential palace and within hours they were calling it Ho Chi Minh City.[xxviii]

On the day South Vietnam was taken over Darryl was in the boozer in Townsville listening to the news on the radio… 'North Vietnamese tanks have smashed into the gates of the palace.'

The war in Vietnam lasted thirty years from 1945 to 1975.

Over those thirty years:

Three million Vietnamese were thought to have died including ARVN, VC, NVA and civilians and 1.5 million people fled Vietnam.[xxix]

An estimated 500,000 Americans had served in Vietnam, approx. 58,000 had died and 90,000 were wounded.[xxx]

Between 1962 and 1972, around 60,000 Australians had served. 521 had died and 3000 were wounded.[xxxi]

A tragic number and a tragic ending.

*History and statistics sourced from the following documentary which we recommend for a full account and history of the Vietnam War - Burns, K. and Novick, L., The Vietnam War, Documentary

Darryl 'Coop' Cooper

Part 6

The Battle After the War

There are times on a dirt road that there is no sound but the hum of the gravel underneath the ute and you can't feel anything because the reverberation of the road through your body replaced all emotion that was once there. Staring through the windscreen you can't hold a thought for there is nothing in front of you nor behind you. The minutes turn into hours and the hours turn into years.

45
The Beginning of a New Chapter

Darryl decided to stay in the army and got a job as a supervisor of the soldiers' mess. 'I would make sure that the soldiers had plenty of good food and make sure that the duties and tasks were carried out.'

After some time, The Royal Australian Infantry Corp Band moved into their lines. Darryl became good friends with them and would drink with them down at the boozer.

He says, 'I actually had my saxophone with me at the barracks. I used to fall asleep on the juke box every night at the boozer.

One night the band corporal, Laurie Lewis says to me, "Cooper, do you like music?"

I said, "I fuckin' love it."

He says, "Can you play anything?"

I say, "You name it, and I can play it."

The next morning the Major wanted to see Darryl and he remembers thinking, 'What the bloody hell have they got me for now?' He hadn't fallen asleep on duty, he wasn't classified as AWOL, he wasn't picked up by the military police. He couldn't think of anything he had done. The major asked him if he wanted to join the band. So, Darryl's career as a bandsman started that day.

Beneath the Southern Cross I Stand

The first time that the band marched around 2RAR with Darryl playing his saxophone, they passed battalion headquarters. He was the only one in the band with one sock down and the boys were hanging out the windows giving him a cheer as they marched past.

"Good on ya, Coop!" "You don't need two socks up!" The CO and RSM, were out watching on and were not impressed.

The band would tour out west playing at different towns. At some towns, they would play with Johnny O'Keefe who was a rock'n'roll singer at the time. They would perform in the afternoon and Johnny O'Keefe would be on that night. On one particular night Darryl and Johnny O'Keefe had a drink together in the saloon bar after a show in Clermont where Darryl had worked out on the stations.

When 2RAR was disbanded and became 2/4RAR Darryl could not go to 2/4RAR as they had a bag pipe band. He was transferred by paper to 1RAR and stayed in the Royal Australian Infantry Corp Band.

Darryl says, 'One day the bandmaster for 1RAR wanted to know who this Corporal Cooper was attached to the Royal Australian Infantry Corp Band. He immediately wanted me to be transferred to the 1RAR band where I stayed for years. I ended up being the drum major, band sergeant and sometimes the bandmaster. We used to do a lot of battalion parades and toured in Butterworth, Malaysia three or four times over the years. That's where I was in hospital when I was shot in the head…what goes around, comes around. I got on well with the Diggers from 1RAR, but it was not the same as my mates from 4RAR and 2RAR.' There is a bond formed in the trenches of a war zone that is unlike any other.

One day in Lavarack Barracks the band from Enoggera came up and they were holding a large parade. The bandmaster asked Darryl to take the sergeants around Townsville for a beer.

"Who better for that job?" he says.

Darryl 'Coop' Cooper

In one of those serendipitous moments that so often happens to Darryl, he was sitting at a table sipping a beer with Sergeant Les Owens, and Darryl asked Les if he agree with National Service.

Les replied, "No, my wife and myself are dead against it."

Darryl asks why and Les explained, "I was teaching a young bloke in Rockhampton how to play the sax and he was a good kid and looked like he had potential. Anyway, he was killed in Vietnam."

Darryl said, "Oh no, poor bastard, what was his name? I might know him?"

Les said "Darryl Cooper."

Darryl pulled out his driver's licence and showed him who he was. Les had taught Darryl about six saxophone lessons before Darryl had joined the army. Les couldn't wait to ring his wife and tell her the news that Darryl was still alive.

After around nine years in the band, Warrant Officer Peter Stewart talked Darryl into going to the quartermaster store. Darryl was tired of touring and sleeping in motels, so he decided to complete the Q Courses.

While completing the course, he got an attack of gout and was admitted to hospital. Darryl's mate from Southern Cross, Ken Swadling, who he joined the army with, was based in Victoria at the time, and heard Darryl was in hospital. Ken paid him a visit. Ken said, 'I tried to pretend I was a doctor and took his pulse. We hadn't seen each other for about fifteen years, and I thought he might not recognise me.' But even after fifteen years Darryl did recognise Ken and he says, 'Ken hasn't changed at all, even now.'

Once he completed his Q Courses Darryl was transferred to the District Support Unit as a staff sergeant. He became Company Quartermaster Sergeant (CQMS) of the unit, which was based in Watsonia, Melbourne. He marched into the sergeants' mess to be supplied with his accommodation and all his gear.

Beneath the Southern Cross I Stand

Darryl says, 'As I entered, there was a sergeant being ordered by a captain. I waited outside until they were finished and who do you think that captain was? It was my mate, Ken Swadling.'

'When I arrived in Watsonia, the soldiers there were from other corps who did not want them. They were coming to work in civilian clothes at any time they wanted. I let it go on for a week or so and then I pounced. I had parades three times a week before their work started inspecting their uniforms, haircuts, boots and anything else I would think of. I used to drill them up and down with rifles. I also had two girls in the platoon which was a first for me. They all became efficient soldiers. But I was not happy at Watsonia for I was there for six months over the winter, and I missed Queensland and my Rugby League Football.'

After twenty years in the Army, Darryl decided to take his discharge. The soldiers threw a going away party for him and presented him with a plaque with all their Corp Badges on it. The plaque read,

'Thanks, Staff, for making soldiers out of us.'

46
Dawn or Dusk

On the 1st of July 1985, Sergeant Darryl Cooper was discharged at Northern Command Personnel Depo (NCPD), Enoggera Army Base, Brisbane. Enoggera, where twenty years earlier he walked into the Australian Army a nineteen-year-old boy, he now walked back out into the world a thirty-nine-year-old man.

It is at the point where a soldier has to walk from the army and war back into the world that he must learn to live in that world all over again. He brings with him the horrors and trauma of what he has been through. Those moments of war that replaced his dreams with nightmares.

There are incidents in life that blindside you. You don't see them coming and the event is so shocking and affects you so deeply that it changes you. Incidences like a car accident or the death of someone you love. These traumatic moments are so shocking that even if you know they are coming you can't do anything to change your reaction or the lasting effect it has on you.

Like soldiers going to war. As prepared as they may be, they never truly knew how they will react at the moment they are shot at. As Darryl said in his first tour, 'Will I run? Will I freeze? Will I protect my mates?' He didn't know how he would react to the fear that took over him as he walked through a jungle with no front line not knowing where the enemy is. Or the fear as he lay in a trench at stand to, head down waiting for shrapnel to hit his body. Or the fear when his gun jammed as he was staring into the eyes of the Viet Cong. How would he react when wounded and on the Dust Off not sure if he would survive? How would he then survive the pain and suffering, through months of rehabilitation confined to a hospital bed with nowhere to hide from the flashbacks?

At the time of trauma, the body goes into fight or flight mode. The adrenaline kicks in and they are on autopilot. Like the moment Darryl went through sixty rounds beside Tom. Once this passes, there is the shellshock…he doesn't remember changing the magazines. Their mind shuts down the event as if it never happened, memories too horrific they must be locked away in a secret compartment forever.

The men who return from war have to battle with these fears, memories and the flashbacks while also grieving for those they have lost. For a time, they might feel numb, then there is the anger, the sadness or the nightmares night after night. When they woke, confused and lost, they could not tell dawn from dusk. Some would turn to alcohol or drugs.

Darryl says, 'Some would commit suicide. Others, their wives would leave them to fend for themselves. We would find it hard to mourn…we had no tears left. We would never be the same again.'

Darryl like many other war veterans suffered this burden of war. It was a shadow that followed him from Vietnam. A shadow that he has fought over the years. At times, drowning it with alcohol. Other times, screaming at it in anger. Sometimes, weeping with it for those he has lost. It was not something that would ever go away but that he would learn to live with. And the shadow was given a name—PTSD.

Darryl 'Coop' Cooper

Often due to the stigma of Vietnam, the soldiers had to face this battle when they returned by themselves.

Darryl says, 'When we came back home, we had to put up with our own citizens who spat on us and called us names that even I could not repeat. But that was one of the main reasons we went to Vietnam so that the people in the South could express their own opinions and have their own elections without interference from the communists of North Vietnam. So, we took the abuse. Don't forget it was the Australian Government that sent us to Vietnam not our generals and who voted the government in? The Australian people.'

A war that was initially supported by the majority of the Australian people had become unpopular and consequently, the government who had sent the men to Vietnam now turned on them. The men were abandoned upon their return.[xxxii] (*Paul Ham's book Vietnam: The Australian War chapter 42 is a must read for an account of the treatment of the returned soldiers.)

It was not until fifteen years after the Vietnam War had ended that a welcome home parade was held in Sydney to recognise our Vietnam Veterans. It was on that day in 1987 that Bob Hawke announced Vietnam Veterans' Day would be the 18th of August. A day to commemorate the men and women who served in Vietnam. A day that lifted the veil and allowed them to admit they were a Vietnam Veteran without the fear of being ostracised.

47
A Final Note From 'Coop'

After returning home to Rockhampton, after Vietnam I had a lot of time to think about my experiences so far. I sat down at a local pub with a XXXX beer and thought about Malaysia, Borneo and Vietnam. Maybe I might get to be a soldier at peace now—that'll never happen. Maybe it is time to look after our own country now. I started off to appreciate all branches of the navy, army and air force for being excellent men and women who looked after us and bought us home safe.

    I thought about all the mums, dads, brothers and sisters and relations who never gave up on us. I thought about the doctors, nurses, the Nui Dat water truck drivers, Signal men and women from Saigon, the entertainment who lifted our moral, the cooks, the medics, the helicopter pilots, the people who supplied and made up our rations, the people who packed the ammunition, the people who made our uniforms and equipment. We were always well-dressed, well-armed and well fed. Thanks everyone who supported us. I could not mention all of you because that would be another book.

    I would also like to take this opportunity to say how professional and responsible the men of my section were. They were excellent soldiers. Also, they knew and carried out the responsibilities they were given. If they were given the job of scout, machine gunner or rifleman it would be efficiently done. I will not mention them here…or I would be afraid to miss out on even one name so I will not name them. They know who they are. Thanks, fellas, for making my job easier. It was also great to have served with B Company 2RAR again.

During the second tour, one of our officers was presented with a Military Cross—Second Lieutenant PN Gibson. Corporal KN Johnson was awarded a Military Medal and Private RK Hawkins was mentioned in dispatches and two years ago was awarded Medal of Gallantry. All men from 6 Platoon B Company.

Back in Rockhampton, I would go outside on a starlit night and look up at the Southern Cross. I would love you to take the time one starry night to look up at the Southern Cross. Picture the Australian flag. Spend a moment remembering our sailors, soldiers and airmen who died fighting for that flag and country. Do not shed a tear because they would not like that. But remember the hard and the sad work they went through. Remember them in your own way; Anzac Day, Memorial Day or Vietnam Veterans' Day or maybe their birthday or their first day at school. Remember in your way. You don't have to be told how to remember.

There is an old saying in the army…
Ours is not to reason why, but to do and die.

I still fight my little battles in Vietnam every day and every night.

May the world ever be a safer place. I don't want to see any of our younger generations have to see what I've seen and go through the things I have gone through.

Now that I am at the end of my story, there is one name that I left until last—Ken Swadling. Thanks, Ken, because we both took that day off at Southern Cross and you talked both of us into joining the army. Otherwise, this story would never have happened. Even though we joined together, we never served together but for my twenty years I always wondered where you were—close or far away from me. I know you always supported me at the front. Ken, thanks for the sad and wonderful twenty years. I stand to attention, tall and salute you. Best of luck in the future my true mate, 'Coop'.

The End

Acknowledgements

The main source of this book is the story told by Darryl Cooper during our weekly discussions and questions recorded on Dictaphone from 8th June 2020 to September 2021. During these fifteen months Darryl spent countless hours writing and unlocking his memories of fifty years ago. Along the way, he needed a little help from his mates who shared the experiences with him. Darryl says, 'Even though they had trouble remembering also.'
We would like to acknowledge the contributions of the following friends.

Mates from the early days and Malaysia:
Ken Swadling
Ken retired after twenty years in the army and settled in Victoria with his wife Denise. He worked for one of the big four banks as Training Manager. He retired early due to health reasons and now lives with his wife Denise in Berwick, Melbourne.

Peter 'Andy' Anderson
After leaving the army Andy moved back to Mitchell where he worked in the local council as a labourer. He worked in hospitals and nursing homes in Dalby for several years and then moved to Roma where he lives now. Darryl visits Andy in Roma whenever he can.

Beneath the Southern Cross I Stand

Roy 'Cleggie' Clegg
Cleggie was on his second tour in Vietnam when he decided to leave the army. He stayed in Sydney for a while then moved with his brothers to Queensland worked picking fruits and at meatworks. He worked in the area of Mundubbera, Bowen and Mackay. He bought a house in Bowen where he stayed for some time while making several trips to Greenslopes Hospital in Brisbane. He sold his home in Bowen and moved to Maryborough. When Darryl was shot in the head during his first tour, Cleggie thought Darryl had died. It wasn't until years later when that they reunited and remained friends until Cleggie passed away.

Robert 'Bob' Frauenfelder
Bob returned out of the army when he arrived back in Borneo. He worked as an engineer on drilling rigs throughout New South Wales. He then moved to Gympie where he started a shed building business. After a few years he moved back to Griffith with his wife. He bought a plane and now flies around the country.

John 'Yogi' Philips
'Yogi was a terrific mate during my hardest army life in Malaysia and Borneo.' After Yogi was discharged from the army he settled in Adelaide where he started a second-hand business called '*Ye Ole Trading Post*'. After living in Adelaide for some time he moved to Smithton in north-west of Tasmania where he started a garbage run and tidied bins. He passed away on the 18th of June 2020. He is now buried at the Circular Heads Cemetery, Tasmania.

Darryl 'Coop' Cooper

Graeme Marshall
Graeme left the army after six years and worked a variety of jobs: butcher, contract boning, management. He took up offshore sailing and sailed the coast of Australia and beyond. He now lives on the coast of New South Wales.

My relatives and friends:
Scott Edward Cooper (son), Val Crawford (sister), Errol Cooper (brother), Lynn Cooper (sister-in-law), Wayne Cooper (cousin), Les Rankin (schoolmate), Bob Burnham (mate), Charlie the Dog (my best furry friend and support), Jo Quadrio (who helped me with the computer and with home care in Gympie)

Thanks for supporting me over those terrible days when I went on leave in Rockhampton, 'Coop'.

Mates from Vietnam 1st tour:
For my first tour in Vietnam, I would like to thank the B Company Veterans for accepting me into their unit. I marched in from a different battalion where we had just finished a tour of Malaya and Borneo. We had different tactics to 2RAR, but we soon settled into their way of life. We were treated no different to from any other recruits that had marched in even though there were about sixty of us. During Vietnam, I got on great with 2RAR and I hope they got on great with me. Not long after we got home and were discharged Ian Atkinson and I started reunions for 2RAR which still happen every two years. The first reunion was at Singleton in 2000. We have all kept in contact since and all remain great mates. May the big general in the sky salute them all.'
Bill 'Billy' Wearne, Stan 'The Man' Jaruga, Chris Cannan, Ian 'Aka' Atkinson, Dave Mansfield, Alan 'Bluey' Jaques, John 'Jock' Cassidy, Sel 'Geoff' Pitt, Robert 'Kloppy' Klopp, Dave Whitehouse,

Beneath the Southern Cross I Stand

George 'Georgie' Duff, Bill 'Super' Dewenger, Denis Wanless, Brian 'Andy' Andrews, Geoff Brewer, Kenny Boaler, Robert Carmichael, Richard 'Dicky' Glenn (Passed away 15 April 2019), Johnny Barnes (Passed away 5 May 2020)

Mates from Vietnam 2nd Tour:
Even though I was in 2RAR (water tank driver), after a couple of months in country, I was asked to get back to rifle company. I marched into 4 Platoon B Company which was my old unit on the first tour. Again, the soldiers of B Company accepted me with open arms and I soon became a commander of a section. Dave Mansfield, Chris Cannan and Jock Cassidy used to try to compare 2nd to 1st tour. We worked mainly in companies and battalion strength on the first tour and on the second tour we only worked in our section, platoon and companies. The Vietnamese government was trying for its own army to take more responsibility. We still had our share of contact with the enemy. What made it worse was we knew what the outcome would become. I was glad I had both experiences.

Dave Mansfield, Chris Cannan, John 'Jock' Cassidy, John Schroeder, Allan 'Pop' Norman (passed away Sept 2021) Bill 'G.M.H' Holden, Pat Brown, Gary Mcdonnell, Alan Farquar, Bill Van Wegberg, 'Cowboy' Jones, Jack Vantongeren, Major G. Hoffman, Lance Corporal Donny Radford
Thanks mates, for getting me through the hardest army days of my life! Thanks for being good soldiers and having me as a friend, 'Coop'.

B Company Officers: Major G. Hoffman (OC), Captain J.R. Black, Captain B. Tons (2IC)

Darryl 'Coop' Cooper

Platoon Commanders: LT P. McNamara (4Pl), LT G. Chasling (5Pl), 2nd LT P.N. Gibson (6Pl)

Up the old Red Rooster!

Beneath the Southern Cross I Stand

This book is dedicated to the memory of Bobby Taylor.

Darryl says, 'It must have been in the early nineties when I was at a 2RAR reunion at the Twin Towns RSL on the Gold Coast. I had been talking and drinking with this bloke for about an hour when he turned to me with a lopsided grin and said, "You don't know who I am, Cooper, do you?" He always called me Cooper. I said, "I would not have a fuckin' clue who you are."

He said he was a scout in Ian Atkinson's 1 Section in Vietnam and then it hit me. It was little Bobby Taylor. In Nui Dat, he would pass our section lines going to Company Headquarters, Platoon Headquarters, the cookhouse mess or to the boozer and would always call in for a chat. From that day on we became best mates. It was always Bobby Taylor, Ian Atkinson and myself. We would go to reunions together and have a fantastic time.

Bobby came from Mansfield in Victoria. He lived at Albert Park for a while, and I would go down and see him. We also did a couple of road trips together which I still have fond memories of.

Bobby would tell everyone that the day I was shot he had set me up and that the people firing at me when I was placed in the stokes litter and winched up into the dust off was him and his mates. He was only joking but loved telling that story.

At one reunion in Geelong, I fell over and got a black eye. Bob told everyone that he king hit me and then everyone shouted him beers for the whole reunion. He ended up drinking UDLs or what I called 'girlie drinks.'

Bobby eventually moved to Maroochydore on the Sunshine Coast and we could get together more often for I had moved up to the Noosa area. He passed away at Nambour Hospital on the 19th of October 2011. He is not only missed by me, but by everyone who knew him.

Darryl 'Coop' Cooper

Darryl 'Coop' Cooper:

When Darryl left the army in 1985, he moved to a property in Calliope, Gladstone. He relocated to Bundaberg in the early nineties and was transferred to Port Curtis Dairy where he worked as Production Manager. This is where he met Michelle in 1992. Michelle says, 'The staff called him "Chief" at work. They all loved him. He had a huge red Valiant at the time and you could hear him coming from a mile away. When he started the Valiant a big puff of smoke would fill the street.'

Later that same year Darryl received a letter forwarded by the Vietnam Veterans' Association. The letter was from Scott—Darryl's son born twenty-six years earlier in 1966 when Darryl was in Borneo.

Scott was told growing up that his father was killed in Vietnam. Darryl says, 'When Scott was eighteen, he was at a party and was talking to his mate's mum. Scott said along the lines of, "It's a pity my old man was killed in Vietnam." His friend's mum knew about me and said, "No, he wasn't killed. He was shot in the head and wasn't expected to live but I think he survived and if he's around he would be in Queensland."'

Eight years later Scott saw the Vietnam Veterans' Memorial open in Canberra on TV and thought he would search for Darryl via the Vietnam Veterans' Association. The Association told Scott to write a letter and they would pass it to the Queensland Vietnam Veterans who were coming to NSW. The letter made it to the Bundaberg RSL and then was sent to Darryl.

When Darryl received Scott's letter, he went straight to the RSL and celebrated with his friends. He says, 'I found out I had two grandchildren, so we got pissed and smoked cigars.' Shortly after the news, Darryl hired a car and drove down to see Scott in New South Wales. He met Scott at the Seven Hills RSL club, which is where twenty-seven years earlier Darryl had met Scott's mum, Carol. Scott was living in the same house that Carol lived in when Darryl was dating her. The same house that Darryl visited in 1968 and from the front door saw two-year-old Scott playing in the living room. Scott and his family eventually moved to Morayfield, Queensland which was not far from Darryl, so they were able to see each other more often over the years.

Port Curtis Dairy closed down in December 1995, and Darryl and Michelle were made redundant. They decided to relocate to the Sunshine Coast. It was at this time when Darryl stopped working that the horrors of war haunted him and his struggle with PTSD began. They bought a house out of town in Cudgerie, Black Mountain near Cooroy where they lived for eighteen years. When Michelle decided to move to Melbourne in 2018, Darryl moved to Gympie. After twenty-six years together, they are still good friends and talk often.

Darryl loves a road trip and over the years you could always find him travelling around Australia in his four-wheel drive covered in Vietnam Vet and Rabbitoh stickers. He is not well now so finds it hard to travel but still hits the road when he can. He lives by himself with his dog, Charlie, in Gympie. He loves the company of friends so when you are nearby, make sure he takes you to Kingston House in Gympie for dinner and a laugh. Trust me, you won't regret it!

As I said in my preface,
'Sometimes in life you come across someone that can brighten your day and make you laugh no matter how terrible you are feeling. Even after all that he has been through and all he has seen, this is a rare gift that Darryl has…maybe it is because of all he has been through and all he has seen.'

Darryl 'Coop' Cooper

Above: Vietnam Veterans Day 18 August 2021, Standown Park, Gympie
Darryl placing a brick on behalf of B Company, 2RAR brick.

Sadly, the B Company 2RAR biennial reunion planned for Gympie was cancelled due to COVID-19.

Photos taken by Leonie Schwartz

Left: Service Medals

Beneath the Southern Cross I Stand

Author - Danielle Ryan

For me, writing Darryl's story was an incredible experience. An experience that I hope readers of Beneath the Southern Cross I Stand also have. It was educational, enlightening and emotional all at the same time. It gave me a greater appreciation of what our service men and women have been through and a better understanding of Darryl's PTSD. I learned his PTSD shadow was always there - it had just changed over the years. While telling his story, Darryl's nightmares returned. He needed a break but was adamant we continued. I think sharing his story somehow helped.

Darryl was very unwell with a lung disease during the time that we were filling my Dictaphone with our conversations. We rushed publishing and I am thankful that he got to hold the final copy of the book in his hands just before he passed away in February 2022.'

All profit from the book is being donated to assist Veterans and their families.

Bibliography

Books:

Appy, C., Vietnam: The Definitive Oral History Told from All Sides, New York, 2007.
Avery, B., Our Secret War Defending Malaysia Against Indonesian Confrontation, 1965-67, Slouch Hat Publications, McCrae, 2001.
Ham, P., Vietnam: The Australian War, Harper Collins, Sydney 2007.
Newman, K., The ANZAC Battalion in Vietnam 1967 – 68, Volume 1, Printcraft Press, Brookvale, NSW, 1968.
Pelvin, R., Vietnam: Australia's Ten Year War 1962 – 1972, Hardie Grant Books, Victoria, 2006.

Studies, reports, essays, articles:
Avery, B., Indonesian Confrontation of Malaysia 1962-1966
Detteer, D. and Underwood, J., A Brief History of the Fourth Battalion of the Royal Australian Regiment (4RAR)

Documentary:
Burns, K. and Novick, L., The Vietnam War

Websites:
4RAR www.4rar2.com
Australian War Memorial www.awm.com.au
National Service www.nashoaustralia.org.au
Royal Australian Regiment www.rarnational.org.au/history
HMAS Sydney http://www.navy.gov.au
https://history.state.gov/milestones/1953-1960/seato

Endnotes

[i] This verse recalled by Darryl was chanted by the Australian Soldiers of 2RAR in the 60s and 70s. This version ended in 'Up the old red rooster and more piss!' The origins of this verse have been debated for decades. It is thought that it was derived from the late 1800s song Australia: Heart to Heart Hand to Hand, Rev. Thomas Hilhouse Taylor. A version of this verse was chanted by the diggers of WW2, another version chanted by the Australian Cricket team from the 70s has become their victory song. Wherever the origins lay, Darryl and I agreed, at the heart of this war cry (if you will) is a patriotism and love of Australia that runs deep in those that chant it.
https://www.australianculture.org/under-the-southern-cross-i-stand/
[ii] https://history.state.gov/milestones/1953-1960/seato
[iii] Pelvin, Vietnam Australia's Ten Year War 1962 – 1972, p.2
[iv] Avery, Indonesian Confrontation of Malaysia 1962 – 1966, p. 1-3
[v] Avery, Indonesian Confrontation of Malaysia 1962 – 1966, p. 3
[vi] Avery, Indonesian Confrontation of Malaysia 1962 – 1966, p. 9
[vii] Avery, Indonesian Confrontation of Malaysia 1962 – 1966, p. 10
[viii] Burns, K. and Novick, L., The Vietnam War, Documentary
[ix] www.rarnational.org.au/history
[x] www.nashoaustralia.org.au/history
[xi] www.navy.gov.au
[xii] Pelvin, Vietnam Australia's Ten Year War 1962 – 1972, p.35-37
[xiii] Pelvin, Vietnam Australia's Ten Year War 1962 – 1972, p.84
[xiv] Newman, The ANZAC Battalion in Vietnam 1967-68 Volume 1 – Operation Geraldton

[xv] Newman, The ANZAC Battalion in Vietnam 1967-68 Volume 1 – Operation Paddington
[xvi] Newman, The ANZAC Battalion in Vietnam 1967-68 Volume 1 – Operation Cairns
[xvii] Newman, The ANZAC Battalion in Vietnam 1967-68 Volume 1 – Operation Atherton
[xviii] Newman, The ANZAC Battalion in Vietnam 1967-68 Volume 1 – Operation Ainslie
[xix] Newman, The ANZAC Battalion in Vietnam 1967-68 Volume 1 – Operation Kenmore
[xx] Newman, The ANZAC Battalion in Vietnam 1967-68 Volume 1 – Operation Sante Fe
[xxi] Newman, The ANZAC Battalion in Vietnam 1967-68 Volume 1 – Operation Forest
[xxii] Newman, The ANZAC Battalion in Vietnam 1967-68 Volume 1 – Operation Forest
[xxiii] Newman, The ANZAC Battalion in Vietnam 1967-68 Volume 1 – Operation Forest
[xxiv] Newman, The ANZAC Battalion in Vietnam 1967-68 Volume 1 – Operation Duntroon
[xxv] Newman, The ANZAC Battalion in Vietnam 1967-68 Volume 1 – Operation Coburg
[xxvi] Newman, The ANZAC Battalion in Vietnam 1967-68 Volume 1 – Operation Coburg
[xxvii] Pelvin, Vietnam Australia's Ten-Year War 1962 – 1972, p.201-206
[xxviii] Burns, K. and Novick, L., The Vietnam War, Documentary
[xxix] Burns, K. and Novick, L., The Vietnam War, Documentary
[xxx] Burns, K. and Novick, L., The Vietnam War, Documentary
[xxxi] Ham, P., Vietnam: The Australian War, Harper Collins, Sydney 2007
[xxxii] Ham, P., Vietnam: The Australian War, Harper Collins, Sydney 2007, P. 560-573

www.ingramcontent.com/pod-product-compliance
Lightning Source LLC
Chambersburg PA
CBHW040241010526
44107CB00065B/2824